Praise for Nob

T0007661

"(Ramos) pulls no punches in analyzing the wellsprings of her adult challenges and childhood angst. . . . She emerges from this reflective process to a new position of power . . . Very highly recommended for anyone interested in self-help strategies, memoirs of abuse and recovery, and those involved in transforming lives from a foundation of abuse to achieve empowerment."

—D. Donovan, Senior Reviewer,
Midwest Book Review

"*Nobody's Daughter* is a lucid recollection of a childhood no one would have chosen. The author's courage as a sexual abuse survivor has an inspiration of its own. Her yearning for her mother's love is heartbreakingly raw. In a fiercely candid voice, Rica has crafted a tale that resonates with the universal truth that our past doesn't define us; it refines us."

—Allison Hong Merrill,
author of *Ninety-Nine Fire Hoops*

"*Nobody's Daughter* is masterfully written. With insight, love, forgiveness, and an evolved understanding, Rica Ramos dives deep into the complexities of mother-daughter relationships as they are woven through real-life ups and downs and the traumas that so many of us must overcome. A compelling read I could not put down. This book will benefit every woman."

—Linda Lee Blakemore, speaker, advocate, and author
of *Entrenched: A Memoir of Holding On and Letting Go*
and *Kids Helping Kids Break the Silence of Sexual Abuse*

"Ramos's imagery is fresh, precise, and strongly drawn. *Nobody's Daughter* is suffused with a beauty as brutal as it is breathtaking. Her memoir is a compelling account of her lifelong journey from unspeakable betrayal and violation to healing and wholeness. She pulls apart and examines with precision the many interwoven layers of love, loss, and lies we live with. Rica is a writer of extraordinary talent, with a gift for bringing clarity to complex issues. Her voice demands to be heard."

—Lee Gaitan, author of *My Pineapples Went to Houston*
and *Lite Whines and Laughter*

NOBODY'S DAUGHTER

A Memoir of Healing the Mother Wound

RICA RAMOS

SHE WRITES PRESS

Published 2023

Printed in the United States of America

Print ISBN: 978-1-64742-491-6
E-ISBN: 978-1-64742-492-3
Library of Congress Control Number: 2022912621

For information, address:
She Writes Press
1569 Solano Ave #546
Berkeley, CA 94707

She Writes Press is a division of SparkPoint Studio, LLC.

Preface

As a young girl, I was obsessed with poetry, with cracked volumes that smelled of dust and neglect, whose yellowed pages were golden treasures in my hands. One day I found a poem I've never forgotten: "She Walks in Beauty" by Lord Byron. Here was a mythical woman, but I knew her the way you know a recurring dream, a déjà vu moment, or a sparkling secret. I wanted her to be possible, to be perfect. Lord Byron savored her beauty and grace, but I hoped for something more.

I imagined she was maternal. She could listen to my stories and throw back her raven tresses and say, "Tell me more." She could nurture me, love me, and choose me over the man who'd abused me, her man. She could be my safe haven, my mother. But this woman was a kaleidoscope of dreams, shimmering fragments of wisdom, warmth, humor, strength, compassion, patience, and love. I romanticized her being, because I needed a heroine. With her image in my mind, I pinned my expectations on my own mother, a woman who didn't have the courage to save me. A woman who could never be flawless.

When I held the poem in my little hands, I held it in my heart too. It would take me three decades to set the woman free, the woman who belonged only to the pages and could never be anything more than Lord Byron's and my fantasy. It's hard to tell a girl that poetry is poetry and mothers—rather, women—are simply people. This book is the story of that journey. It is the untangling of a myth, the revelation of the truth about women and mothers. It is a narrative about imperfect beauty, because it's the only kind that ever existed.

She Walks in Beauty

by Lord Byron

She walks in beauty, like the night
Of cloudless climes and starry skies;
And all that's best of dark and bright
Meet in her aspect and her eyes;
Thus mellowed to that tender light
Which heaven to gaudy day denies.

One shade the more, one ray the less,
Had half impaired the nameless grace
Which waves in every raven tress,
Or softly lightens o'er her face;
Where thoughts serenely sweet express,
How pure, how dear their dwelling-place.

And on that cheek, and o'er that brow,
So soft, so calm, yet eloquent,
The smiles that win, the tints that glow,
But tell of days in goodness spent,
A mind at peace with all below,
A heart whose love is innocent!

Chapter 1

A Dress

A mannequin wore a bridal gown in the store window. The tall, svelte plastic form flaunted a fairy-tale figure. I thought about this when I spent more time on fitness. My heart thundered a storm in my chest as I ran faster and longer. Sweat stained my sports bra, and I planked until my arms shook and burned. Still, my body was not svelte. I'm short and have actual hips. That dress in the window wouldn't work for me.

More than a decade post-divorce, Wes was the man who made me want to wear a wedding dress again. But I had been to all the local venues and scoured some thrift shops, too, without finding the right one for me. Musty little stores with rumpled dresses askew on plastic hangers. I liked the idea of wearing something with a history, a dress with experience. Because I am a woman with experience. But wedding dress shopping had flipped a switch in my brain. I saw magazine model brides in designer dresses and boutique mannequins sporting teeny dresses, and it made me feel worn, like an old pair of jeans. I plucked satin and lace from store racks, but every dress made me feel frumpy. Why did I suddenly feel like the self-critical girl of my youth?

I parked my car and worked up the nerve to enter the bridal shop, eyeing the mannequin as if to challenge her. The glass door banged shut behind me, and a bell jingled. A sixtyish woman looked up from the counter and smiled, holding up a finger in a "one minute" sign. She cradled the telephone on her shoulder and scribbled on a legal pad. Her white-yellow hair was upright and oblong shaped, a butterfly net in the wind. She had a substitute school teacher look, and I thought of Mrs. Lamen at the front of my fifth-grade classroom in her polyester pantsuit and stodgy, drugstore eyeglasses. When she finished the call, I learned she was Mary, the store owner.

"Are you the bride?" she asked, followed by, "When is the wedding? What is your budget? How many guests? Have you chosen a venue? What size do you wear? What style do you like—traditional, sexy, elegant?"

"Ahh . . . umm. . . ." I began, then took a deep breath. "I like lace. Mesh sleeves, maybe—a vintage look."

"Beautiful. Yes, that will be perfect for you, honey. Just perfect, honey," she said, clasping her hands like a prayer. She held out a questionnaire. "Fill this out and I'll order something special for you to try on."

I stood there with the clipboard for a while until I had checked every box on the form. When I finally handed her my paperwork, she was giddy. We set an appointment for Saturday afternoon.

"Honey, you're going to love the dress," she said as I headed for the door.

When Saturday came, my friend Suhaill met me in the parking lot. We are soul-mate friends, the kind who can finish each other's sentences, not talk for many months, and then talk again as if no time has passed. She is a quick-talking Cuban woman with copper-dyed hair and soft brown eyes. We met nearly a decade ago in an office where she was a magazine manager, and I had applied for a job.

"You're a writer?" This was more a statement than a question. Her legs crossed, one peep-toe high heel tapped on the carpet in the conference room. When she asked about my family, I told her I was divorced with two sons named KJ and Sym, and she said she was also a single mom raising a boy. We synced up instantly, the way two shoes fit in a box. One left, the other right. But a pair nonetheless. We were divorced mothers bonded by hardship, motherhood, humor, and fashion. We spent the rest of the interview comparing notes. *Your son does karate? Where do you take him?*

It was the first interview in which I had left with a friend, a job, and no questions as to whether I'd fit in. Suhaill was my first friend in a new state, since I had moved from Wisconsin to Florida with my sons, a packed car, our obese cat, and a whole lot of nerves.

Now, at the bridal shop, the sun washed over the windows and danced on beaded bodices, sequined straps, and belts that looked like swanky necklaces.

"Oh, look at that. Now *that* would look great on you," Suhaill said, pointing to a mermaid dress. "This is A-line, that's a ball gown, and they call this a sweetheart," she said, pointing to all the displays. "You're gonna have to try them all on to see how you feel."

We approached the door, and she'd already cataloged the inventory. She was a drill sergeant, making lists and sending rapid-fire texts with questions, suggestions, photos, and links. *Look at this centerpiece. Check out this sign-in book. What about* the bouquet—silk flowers, baby's breath, tulips, roses, daisies? My wedding was her wedding because I'd enlisted her help. And when she is in, she's all in. It was overwhelming, yes, but it was what I'd asked for, what I needed to help me sort through the endless details. All the while, I wished I could just Rooms-to-Go the wedding. Or pick from a drive-through menu. *Give me the number five please, with a side of eucalyptus.*

Inside the salon, I saw Mary in the center of a cackling female crowd. They were high on wedding-day bliss, tickled by champagne bubbles. A young bride sauntered out of the dressing room, shy in a sheath of a gown. It fit her like a silky new skin. The girl glowed as she stood facing the mirror. Backlit by sunshine, her edges were golden as if drawn with a sunbeam. Her entourage squealed compliments. "Amazing . . . gorgeous . . . stunning. You're a princess."

Two older women stood behind the bride-to-be, and I knew instantly which was her mother. I couldn't see the woman's face, only her hands, as she fussed with her daughter's hair and the fabric of her dress. I meandered around the store racks and feigned interest just to get a better look at this mother and daughter. I was mesmerized by them, by their easy touches and easy banter. This was a foreign language to me, the language of mothers and daughters. With my own mom, there was only shallow conversation and the invisible burden of things left unsaid.

Suhaill caught up with me, holding a dress made of delicate tulle and lace overlays. She thrust it at me. "Look," she said.

"Too frilly," I responded. She snorted and walked away.

It occurred to me that Suhaill is a mother hen, although she's almost exactly my age. Most of my friends are far older, approximately the age of my mother. If I picked this apart, I'd see the obvious psychology. I was attempting to fill a void, to meet a primal need. I gravitated toward those older women because they were maternal and wise. They were mothers to their own children, and they understood what it meant to love a daughter. To protect and preserve the sacred bond.

As I watched the ladies at the bridal shop make a vital memory, savoring the sweetness of a milestone day, I thought about where my mother might be right then. I imagined her sipping her third cup of coffee in front of the television. Her husband on the adjacent sofa, the man she had chosen to love and keep despite the wicked things he did to her children. He was the reason I hadn't asked Mom to come that day. Experience had taught me she'd rather be home with him.

When Mary cheered, I turned away to look for Suhaill. The bride-to-be twirled in another gown, and the squeals began again. After twenty minutes, I was growing impatient. When Mary finally came over, she flashed a smile.

"Yes, honey?" she said, and I thought for a moment she remembered me. But then she asked, "Who is the bride?" And "Do you have an appointment?" And "When is the wedding? What is your budget? How many guests? Have you chosen a venue? What size do you wear? What style do you like—traditional, sexy, elegant?"

I told her I had filled out the forms. "I've been here before. Remember, last week?"

She stared at me blankly when I told her she'd ordered a dress for me, and it was apparent she hadn't. I wondered if she had forgotten, or if the special dress was simply a sales pitch. I'd been looking forward to my appointment all week, imagining the dress that would end my search. Now, I felt duped. Still, I told myself to give Mary a break; perhaps she was just overworked.

"The forms?" I said again, thinking a paper trail might lead her back to me. But she was not interested.

"You're going to be a beautiful bride," she said, pouring on a sugary smile. "Look at your shape, honey. You're petite, aren't you?" She pawed at my waist, smoothing down my sweater to feel the size of me. She walked over to a dress rack. "Look here, honey," she said. "What's your budget?"

We were three honeys in, and I was not feeling too sweet. Suhaill shifted at my side. She nose-breathed, my Darth Vader friend.

"We have a payment plan, if budget is a problem," Mary said. Her eyes arched as if to ask the question again. Budget? Budget? Budget?

"Well, I don't really have a budget . . . I mean. . . ." I fumbled with my words. Mary's eyes brightened at the mention of *no budget*.

I was frustrated now.

"Let's start with these." Mary took my arm and urged me toward the Cadillac rack, the high-priced dresses with hand-stitched Swarovski crystals. We'd seen these gowns elsewhere, and I had come here to find something different. This shop had felt like a last resort. Not a thrift store, but not a swanky boutique either. Mary pulled down gaudy dresses and held them under my chin. She had dollar signs in her eyes.

I thought again of the week I'd spent waiting for a special dress that didn't exist. Suhaill shot me a look, and her mutual annoyance felt like fuel—permission to explode.

"I don't want these dresses, and I don't have a budget problem," I said, swatting away the ten-pound sparkling gown she held up, which looked more like a chandelier than the vintage dress I'd envisioned. "I want my paperwork. I want the dress you promised me."

Mary looked at me like I had slapped her. Her hands fell slack at her side. Fifteen minutes later, Suhaill and I were soaking our pancakes in syrup at the diner across the street, a truck-stop kind of place with career waitresses, gray-haired and aproned. They knew customers by name, but called everyone *darlin'* anyway. Suhaill picked up a curl of bacon. "I guess this is my cheat meal," she said. "Screw it."

"So, you're not vegan or low-carb or paleo or . . . whatever today?"

"Who can be vegan when we're planning a wedding?" she snapped, then laughed her floaty, schoolgirl laugh. "I'm a stress eater, girl. You know bacon is a food group for me."

I laughed too. Then we went silent as we worked on our pancakes. In between bites, we glanced out the window. It was a typical bright day in Florida—heavy with heat, like the weight of emotions. The restaurant was cool and clamoring with old married couples, and bearded men clutching coffee and waiting for plates of hot breakfast meats, their noses in newspapers— the sports section or the automotive page.

Our waitress set a small dish of half-and-half cups on the table, and I thought of my oldest nephew as a child. How he had bitten through all the tiny, sealed cups of creamer at a Denny's restaurant and sucked out the liquid. His plump lips dotted white, he'd turned to me, brown eyes swollen with delight. "Is this baby milk, Auntie Wica?"

I thought of this every time I ate out, and of how he always ordered "macon" because he couldn't say bacon, and this made every waitress adore him. Three years later, my own son came along, and then two years after that, his brother. So many diners. So many messy tables, littered with little sucked-out creamer cups, half-eaten jelly packages, and straw wrappers, twisted and wet. Big tips were a kind of apology, a peace offering

I'd leave behind. My life's work was a series of peace offerings. I was nothing if not a peacemaker, but things were changing. *I* was changing.

Suhaill stared across the table at me. She tilted her head as if waiting for permission to speak.

"What?" I asked.

". . . talk to your mom?"

"No. I just want to focus on this dress. Can we just tackle one problem at a time?"

"Of course," she said. "I don't need you turning into bridezilla."

After our meal, we said our goodbyes in the parking lot. I headed toward my car and pulled my sunglasses from the top of my head to the bridge of my nose. In the car, I kicked my shoes off and massaged the soles of my feet as Suhaill's words echoed in my mind. I put my car in gear, drove to the edge of the parking lot and negotiated a left turn onto the road. *Did you talk to your mom?* She'd asked, and I'd deflected. The thought of Mom split me in two: part woman, part girl. My adult self said focus on finding a dress, being a bride, and living out my happily ever after. But my teenage self haunted me from the streets of Milwaukee. I thought of the warm spring day I'd walked several miles to Southridge Mall after cashing the paychecks I'd earned at my first job, a donut shop. I was sixteen and determined to find the perfect Mother's Day gift for Mom. I thought something extravagant would impress her. When I saw the jewelry store, I headed inside to study the rows of twinkling stones in glass cases. I passed the bridal bands, the solitaires, and cluster rings with bouquets of tiny diamonds.

"What can I help you find?" a young saleswoman had asked me. She set her manicured hands on the counter while I scanned the jewelry buffet.

"These," I'd said, gesturing toward a velvet tray of rubies below the glass. Pear-shaped, oval, heart cuts, and slender marquis stones. Mom's birthstone was not a ruby, but the red jewels conveyed a message I struggled to understand, feelings I'd only grappled with on paper and couldn't articulate outside of the poems I wrote while alone in my bedroom. But Mom wasn't much of a reader; poetry wasn't her language. So I chose a ruby with a slim gold band and carried the little box home in my palm. The sun cast shadows on the sidewalk as I held the gem like a sparkling secret, the bleeding heart of a wounded daughter. The peacemaker.

At home, I told Wes, "It shouldn't be this hard," when he asked how the shopping went. I relayed my experience and the full conversation with Mary. "Honey, honey, honey," I mocked. "What a racket!"

I realized I had pinned my frustrations on Mary, but Wes was my avid supporter. He picked up his iced tea, took a swig, and then held the glass like a thinking prop. "Do whatever you feel comfortable doing. This is your dress," he said. Wes is a lot of things, most importantly, patient.

To the internet I went. . . .

At five in the morning, Wes was at work. Six days a week, he rose early and pulled on his collared shirt and khaki pants in the dark, careful not to wake me. He is a golf man, not in love with the game but rather the challenge of maintaining the course. Monitoring the weather patterns, adjusting irrigation levels, managing the labor and the grounds. Biology, science, and budget—his areas of expertise. But Wes doesn't just care about numbers. He cares about people too. I saw it when he scribbled reminders on sticky notes: *Pick up donuts for the crew.* When he handwrote messages for his staff on the Christmas cards we scoured the aisles of Target to find. When someone stole lunches from the employee break room, his sense of justice took over. I watched his face change as his brain kicked into conflict-resolution mode, his private world of checks and balances. Wes measures life in columns, based on what's true, fair, and practical.

For as long as I'd known him, I'd seen he was all of these things. It didn't take me long to learn that, although I wasn't initially attracted to Wes—not in a dramatic, butterflies-and-lightning-bolts way. But this was a relief for me because experience had taught me that flaming-hot love can fizzle out with a gust of wind. My affection for Wes grew from a foundation of trust, which he'd carefully laid over time—one act of kindness after the other. Little things, like checking my tires, clearing the dishes, arriving on time, and sending quick messages throughout the day. His stability, reliability, and consistency cast a safety net around my anxious heart. If women fall for men like their fathers, I'd done it better by loving a man like my grandfather. When I watched Wes in the dim early morning, so focused and content, I thought of Grandpa whistling songs as the boxed radio played on a shelf in the kitchen. The world was still a sleepy black chasm when Grandpa rose to work his two jobs every day. Like Wes, Grandpa never grumbled about work. He was easygoing and easy to be with.

On my second date with Wes, he'd reached across the table to butter a wedge of bread for me, and that familiar act sealed the deal. I thought of the way Grandpa had sat beside me in the kitchen with a mug of coffee and a morning paper, slathering grape jelly on Saltine crackers and setting the messy bits on my highchair. The back of his hand was sticky with my little-girl handprints. Wes was the same sort of loving companion, a man I trusted instinctively. Being with him was natural, a dance like the one I shared with Grandpa when he pulled me up on the tops of his shoes and held my hand.

In our early weeks of dating, I had driven to Wes's house during a storm, my windshield wipers thrashing madly back and forth. I pulled into his driveway, and in the gray fog outside my car, I saw Wes's silhouette beneath the cover of a black umbrella. When I opened my door, he held it out above my head. I knew then that he was not one to flatter with long-stemmed roses—that was my ex-husband's game. Wes was a man who would keep me safe and dry. After five years together, he still refilled my glass with water when I looked parched. He pushed the cart as we shopped for groceries, and kissed my sleepy face before leaving for work. These little favors sweetened my life like grape jelly on Saltine crackers.

Now the darkness pressed up against our windows as I gazed through the blinds to the moonlit backyard. I saw the white streak of our dog, Mia, her nose in the grass as she sniffed out the path of creeping night critters, taking roll call of the previous shift. I sat down and continued my internet search. "Honey" had a plan. I refused to set foot in another wedding dress shop. I scrolled through photos of wedding dresses with tight-lipped determination. I pored over photos, reviews, and product descriptions before ordering three contenders: a lacy number with a fringed hem, flapper style, a boho chic gown with a flowy skirt and an intricate row of buttons snaking along the back, and a creamy champagne dress with vintage appliqué flowers. I hit the "buy now" button and took a deep breath.

The first two dresses were duds. One was shockingly white, and the other was as stiff as a doily. But on Saturday, the last package arrived while Wes was at work. Perfecto. I'd just try it on while I was home alone. I sliced the box open with scissors and unzipped the plastic bag. *This looks promising.* The fabric was thick and ornamental with a silky liner sewn beneath layers of lace and tulle. *Oh, baby! You could be the one . . .* I ripped off my T-shirt and pulled down my yoga pants. I held up the dress and smiled at my bedroom mirror. *Yes, yes, yes.* With a gentle tug, the zipper came down and I stepped inside the dress. I shifted, twisting and angling to pull the zipper up. It got tricky around my upper back, so I bent my arm from the other direction and shimmied my way inside. I had it now. I adjusted the breast cups and took in the sight of me: rich, elegant, bridal. I was a bride, and this was my dress. I spun, dipped, spun again, then rushed to the closet to grab a pair of heels. I walked in front of the mirror. A wedding walk, slow and intentional. I imagined my sons at my side and pinched back a few proud tears. *This is really happening.* After I'd snapped a few selfies to send to Suhaill, I felt the heat of too much fabric in my sun-soaked bedroom. *Now to get this thing off.*

It was stuck. I rounded my back to smooth the path for the zipper, but I couldn't reach it. I tried to push it down at the neck and grab it from below with the other hand, but it was useless. It would not budge. I needed another arm, or maybe a longer one. An Inspector Gadget arm. It got hotter as I fussed with the zipper, and I began panicking. My palms were slippery as I drew up the hem and pulled the fabric overhead. The dress turned inside out as I yanked it from above. I was buried in layers of lace and tulle. My breath shot out like flames inside my ominous dress-cave. This was the stuff of nightmares. I hyperventilated. I imagined the headline: *Florida Woman Suffocates Herself with Wedding Dress.* I tugged the fabric back down and flopped onto the bed. Deep breath. Deep breath. Deep breath. I stood up again and gave it another go. It felt like hours later, but it was probably more like fifteen minutes when my fingers finally manipulated the zipper from just the right angle. I heard the groan of metal teeth gliding down the fabric track and it sounded like a spiritual hymn. Hallelujah, I am free!

When Wes came home two hours later, I greeted him at the door and announced, "I have found my dress!" This dress and I—we wouldn't hold grudges.

Chapter 2

The Guest List

Memories can be like sandspurs—the thorny parts stick to the skin. Trauma can live in the body; the energy is stored in the tissues, the muscles, and the fascia. I felt it moving through me when Mom talked about my stepdad. My fingers curled into my palms when she said, "Dad." I thought of all the ways he wasn't a dad. The things he did that a dad should never do.

He was playful at first, and when he tickled my little brother, older sister, and me, we tumbled around like puppies on the living room floor. We were giddy, red-cheeked with messy hair and enormous smiles. What a thrill to have an adult playmate. Mom never played like that. She wasn't one for games. But our stepdad's games grew dark in a hurry, and that's when I learned to read the danger signs, the desire in his eyes and body. I sensed acidic notes in the low rumble of his laughter. The way it percolated in his chest, thick like burnt coffee.

I knew when games were just games, and when he had something more sinister in mind. I could feel the subtle shift, like a change in temperature. He was especially bold at night, and on summer afternoons when we swam in the sun-dappled pool. Beneath the water, I liked to watch my hair ripple around me like fronds of seaweed. I could be a graceful mermaid, but when he moved toward me, the fairytales faded and there was his hand. He grabbed my crotch, fondled my flat chest, and my body froze. My legs kicked up as if by reflex. I rocketed to the surface like a firecracker lit by a flame. When I looked around, he was floating beside me, a man-shark, slow and menacing.

My siblings clutched the ledge on the other side of the pool, playing the underwater tea party game. Mom sat on a lawn chair in the grass, sucking the end of a cigarette. Her shoulders shone with oil, and she threw back her head to feel the warmth of the sun. Curls of smoke wafted above her head.

In third grade, I watched an after-school special about molestation. *Tell an adult, a teacher, a neighbor, or someone you trust,* the narrator urged. I thought how easy the narrator made it seem, but how difficult it really was to say such awful things out loud. I thought that if I weren't a girl being touched by her stepdad, I would have no idea how hard "just tell" could be. When I sat on the sofa with Grandma, the picture window framed her backyard, and the green grass was tinged golden with sun, it seemed too perfect a place to bear my story. When I opened my mouth to speak, the words stayed lodged in my throat.

At home in bed, his silhouette jolted me awake, and I felt his hot breath at my bedside, his hand creeping beneath my blankets. My heart sped up in the black abyss. But I squeezed my eyes shut and remembered that this could be just like a story. And stories could have happy endings.

On school days, I clung to books in the library. I sat between rows of metal bookcases. Books, books, books—my alternate universe. The library was lit with fluorescent squares in the ceiling, and walls of windows showed piles of fresh snow on the asphalt parking lot outside. I could disappear inside the displays of new books with soaring dragons on their covers, or creeping caterpillars, ballerinas, and rainbow fish. In later years, I'd found Emily Dickinson's poem about hope—*the thing with feathers that perches in the soul and sings an enduring song*. I prayed for hope, but the bird in my soul stayed silent, unable to coax its voice.

I was around five when the touching began, and in the middle of fifth grade, it finally ended when a friend's mother called the school. My friend had spent the night at my house while my older sister, Jesse, was away for the weekend. I took Jesse's bed, and my friend took mine. In the dark that night, my stepdad slithered in and found her as I slept, touched her the way he'd touched me. She wasn't a shy girl, and her mother was a hefty woman with a booming voice. I often rode in the backseat of their family car, watching the street lamps as we whizzed by on our way back from roller-skating or church youth group functions. Her mother cranked the radio and sang along unapologetically in a voice that was throaty and wild. My friend could be loud like her mother, but she was silent that night in my bed. I wonder if the shock of my stepdad's hands zapped her like a fork in a socket, rendering her numb and listless. That evening, I wasn't aware that he'd touched her, but neither was I surprised to learn it happened.

My stepdad was interested in all the neighborhood kids, always poking into my bedroom to ask questions, his breathing slow and sultry. I hated how he looked at my friends, how he told dumb jokes, or asked lots of questions and laughed like a hungry hyena. The oily smell of his hair as he raked it with one hand and leaned in to watch while we played nervously, aware of his awkward presence. Sometimes he lit a cigarette and just stood there, eyeing us as he inhaled and blew smoke up toward the ceiling. Sometimes he suggested what I might do with my dolls—spread their legs or stack them on top of each other.

"What do you think about this?" he'd asked. His smile sharpened to a cynical point as he rubbed his thumbs on the doll's plastic body. I felt my mouth dry out, my throat cinched as if pulled with a rope.

Aside from the friends he'd touched, there was Erin, a blue-eyed girl I trusted enough to tell my secret. Some weekends when I spent the night at Erin's house, she made pancakes from a box of Bisquick, and I marveled at her ability to just get up in the morning and cook. To spill Bisquick on the counter and not worry about the repercussions. Her mother was a different kind of woman. Erin's pancakes were golden and doughy, and we poured big glasses of orange juice and chugged them at the kitchen table as we ate. We found markers and pens in a drawer and wrote friends' names on our blue jeans. Then we headed outside.

Erin had a tidy backyard and a wooden playhouse her father built. Inside, it smelled like fresh lumber. We were playing in that wooden house when I said, "My stepdad takes off his clothes when we're alone." I kept my eyes on her little dog, Abbey, a beautiful white terrier. "He makes me . . . play games," I continued. I couldn't think of another way to say it. But she knew what I meant. She'd been around him enough to see he was not like her father, Joe, a friendly trash collector who brought home vintage finds—kewpie dolls and household goods that were perfectly useful.

Erin paused, and I felt dread rising up from my bones. I don't know what she said then, but later she'd apologized for lying to the police when they came to her home to ask what she knew about him back in fifth grade. They'd visited a handful of my friends when the school got involved, and I forgave Erin for lacking the courage to say what she knew. She couldn't have known how things would turn out, that even my mother would deny it. That when I turned to her for some kind of warmth or compassion, her hard eyes would yield nothing.

My siblings and I were sent to stay with our grandparents while the authorities sorted things out. In three decades, I'd learn that Mom kept my stepdad with her because we weren't allowed to be near him. She didn't want to send him away, not to a hotel or to his parents' house, where he might have to provide a story. So at night, my sister slept beside me in my grandparents' dark-paneled guest room, my brother in a twin bed near the window. After Grandma tucked us in, I stared at the dim light she left on in the hall, imagining it was a slow-burning ember, a campfire in the cozy woods. We could pretend this was a vacation, a trip to some magical forest.

In the morning, we ate shredded wheat biscuits, corn flakes, or rice puffs, and I stared out the front window as I thought of Mom at home with that man. Perhaps they were the ones on a magical vacation. Was Mom thinking of us? I wanted her near me as I had on my first day of school. I felt the ache and the fear of our separation. I was eleven then, but in Grandma's shower, I cried like a baby as the warm water carried my tears. An intense, overwhelming loneliness throbbed within me, and I felt my face flush. I could smell Mom's perfume, and I imagined the day she'd left us, the red tint of her dyed hair as she'd stepped into her car, pulling the door shut. The sound of it slamming like a door in her heart. I'd never find the key to that door. But I couldn't stop myself from trying.

Sometimes Mom visited, but she didn't stay for more than a few minutes.

I could see her discomfort and sense her irritation, even when she tried to be kind. She said, "When you come home, we'll all go to the pumpkin farm," and I thought about who she meant by "all." I knew she was making plans that included the man. I didn't want to see him again. I'd prayed Mom would send him away. Our closest aunt, Rachel, offered Mom financial help in addition to picking us up from school on Fridays and taking us for weekend sleepovers.

"A lot of women are single mothers. You can do this," she'd pleaded with Mom. "I'll help you. Just leave him."

But Mom refused. And I wondered if she'd even considered it. Did she lie awake at night and mentally pack her things or rehearse some kind of breakup spiel? Was she angry like she'd been when my father stayed out drinking or stumbled in drunk and ornery? Did she think, maybe, because her new husband wasn't prone to drunken rages, the relationship was salvageable after all? Did she think her children were terrible liars? The things he had done for years in secret were now visible in the light of day. But somehow, Mom couldn't, or wouldn't, see it.

When Mom took us to court-ordered counseling sessions, I gazed at her like a mythic creature. She was lovely, pink-lipped, and silent in a chair across the room. I could stare long and hard at her because she kept her eyes averted, as if we were strangers. Perhaps it was the fact that she was always unavailable that made me want her more. Mom clutched the purse in her lap like a shield, and all I had was the scent of her: hairspray, perfume, chewing gum, and the faint smoky shroud of her cigarettes. The sound of her high heels tapping on the floor. I don't know if I expected her to cry when she heard me tell the counselor the things her husband had done, but she never did.

My child self longed to see Mom's sorrow, to watch her face give way to outrage, her lip quiver under the weight of sadness. I needed to know my pain mattered. I mattered. Instead, I saw that what mattered most to Mom was my stepdad. Pretending to be a family was almost the same as being one.

Mom brought us home when the court system gave the okay a few months later. We went back to our bedrooms, put our clothes in our cramped closets, and slept in our old bunk beds. But the house felt like foreign territory. We ate dinners at the dining table in near silence, with only the sound of forks scraping plates. My stepdad sneered at the head of the table. He would spend the rest of my childhood making me and my siblings pay for the trouble we'd caused. And if it was hard to know how to live with our abuser, Mom was there to hand us a script.

There'd be no talk of my real father, no talk of our problems at home. And this is how we all became wonderful actors. I learned to pretend the man was just an innocuous character on the stage of my mother's play. But there were times when I caught him staring at me or breathing in a way that snapped my memory awake. When I lay in bed some evenings, I startled in the dark and imagined him hovering over me. I saw his body in the ominous black of my bedroom, shifting like an animal in the night, creeping upon its prey. But it was always just a memory, and memories were forbidden in my mother's home.

Eager to build my own life, I was married at eighteen and under twenty on the eve of my first anniversary. I'd draped an antique lace tablecloth over a rickety card table, placed a votive candle in a glass, and waited to light its wick. I rocked my infant son, KJ, to sleep, hummed a song in his ear, and let his baby-oiled hair tickle my lips. When sleep claimed his body, softening his limbs like the sweet sprawl of summer, I set my boy down and pulled a blanket up to his chin. I hurried into the bathroom and showered. I played with my makeup and hair, straightening the dark kinks with a fat curling iron, and watching the steam rise from the heated jaw as I pressed my hair flat and glossy. I pulled my wedding dress from the back of the closet, where I'd stored it all year. A simple white garment with a crisscross neckline and a slit from the ankle to the knee. A department store dress, it was all I could afford then, but it was good enough. Like everything else I would settle for.

I'd saved two slices of our wedding cake, wrapped them carefully in plastic and foil, and kept them in the freezer. But that night, I placed them on vintage china plates with pink flowers circling the rim. We'd been married one year, but in my mind there were decades ahead of us. Didn't we promise forever? Wasn't this man my escape, the one who could give me the happy home I'd always wanted? I sat near the window upstairs, watching the street for my husband's car. His shift would end at eleven, and he'd lumber up the steps, work jeans sagging from his tired body. He'd see me in my wedding dress, my straight hair and made-up face. He'd smile, his full lips parting to reveal the pearls of his perfect teeth. His black eyes glazed with surprise, the glow of the votive candle flickering in his eyes, a light I thought would never dim.

But I was naïve.

He didn't come home that night. I'd sat by the window until the dawn pushed its pink haze through the sky, a smoky pastel rising. I'd stripped off my dress and tossed it on the floor when our baby fussed to be fed again. I put on my nightgown and picked up our son, my face a muddy swirl of makeup and tears.

The cake was now stale, the candle burned down to a sooty shell. When my husband arrived in the early morning, he said he'd been scouring the city for a place to buy flowers; but he'd shown up empty-handed. It was the first of many nights that ended this way, and yet I chose to believe the lies. Pretending was the best I could do. It was what I knew from experience, from the mom who'd built our lives on lies. A week later, I put on lipstick again, styled my hair, and took our precious new baby to the mall for family photos. Perhaps I needed the proof of us as a family, the paper sheen of our smiles, our togetherness frozen in time, then framed and hung on a wall. I wanted us to be picture-perfect.

A cheery young woman with a camera posed my husband with baby KJ in his arms. I smiled as I watched his large hands cradle the tender bones of our baby bird. As we passed him around for the shots, the click of the camera jerked his body. His little arm poked up like a scuba tube from the deep ocean of infant slumber. And then the camera turned to me. So enamored of my child, I had forgotten for a moment all the baby weight, my too-round cheeks and swollen body. *Click, click,* I smiled. *Click, click,* I cocked my head at the photographer's prompt. When the proofs were ready a week later, I winced when I saw the funhouse mirror version of myself. Was this why my husband pulled away? I ordered only the photos that didn't include me and went home in a state of shock. *How could that be me?* I'm not sure if postpartum hormones made the experience more devastating, or perhaps too much had changed too fast. I was merely a girl, married with an infant. When I didn't recognize my own face, it was disorienting.

At twenty-two, I had my second son, Sym. KJ was a toddler, and my marriage wasn't quite a marriage. As life got harder, I experienced a loss of gravity. What had I gotten myself into? With one car between us, I waited for my husband to get home so I could take my turn driving to work. At a health center, I learned to bathe the elderly people, to push bedpans beneath their limp bodies and monitor their skin for decubitus ulcers—pressure sores. I had been checking the classifieds in the paper when I saw the ad for health training. I was in the habit of doing this, checking the want ads. A deeper part of me lay in a perpetual state of want, scanning the flimsy paper for something that might dull the ache. Or, at the very least, provide a worthy distraction. When I saw the advertisement, I pictured my grandmother slumped and gray, fogged with Alzheimer's disease, an alternate version of the lively woman who'd sung me songs, fed me sweets, and sat with me in the shade of her pine trees as the birds squabbled overhead. Now she was just a nursing home patient who'd once been a matriarch—like so many others.

I learned to turn bodies on hospital beds and slather them gently with ointments. I kept a taut smile when patients were looking so they couldn't read disgust on my face. The sharp smell of oozing wounds turned my stomach. I learned to tolerate all the odors: urine-soaked sheets, colostomy bags, little pink basins filled with vomit. As I walked the hallways on my shifts, the noise became common too: the hum of oxygen concentrators and infusion pumps as they dispatched relief to patients through plastic tubes. Some nights there were cries for pain medications, wailing, or pleas to Mother Mary. In those halls, I learned the chant of Catholic devotees: *Holy Mary, Mother of God, pray for us*. I heard the subtle click of rosary beads.

One night, I leaned in to help a woman on a low bed, and she reached up abruptly, grabbed a lump of my hair, and yanked me to the ground. The tiny woman with arms like knotty branches, was confused and babbling, "Let me out! Let me out!" Her blue eyes suddenly stormy with flashes of desperation. I struggled to free myself from her grip without snapping her fingers off. I hollered to the staff, and a beefy nurse stormed in, yelling, "Agnes, stop it, now! Agnes, let her go!" And she did. But as soon as Agnes released me, she swung a bony fist at the nurse's face. I watched the nurse's glasses fly across the room and bounce on the linoleum floor.

Alone in the nursing home bathroom, I cried a muted cry. It was the start of my healthcare career, in which I advanced to other roles that paid more but left me empty, drained. At the end of my shifts, I felt guilty and sad. Guilty for being so relieved as I escaped the building like a prisoner who had got-ten a hold of the keys.

The fresh air hit me like a change of seasons. But I was sad for the way of dying, the way bodies wrinkled and bones creaked, the loneliness and the slow pace of suffering. Always, I longed for the chance to write because words were my only ointment. My only bandage. I remembered Mom's stoic face on the day we sat in counseling, and it stirred a monstrous rage in me. But I had been through enough now to know that mothers were good at hiding tears, at crying into pillows at night, and filling their cupped hands with secret salty rivers. After fights with my husband, I had a sense I could finally feel what Mom might have felt—the frustration, the confusion, and the urge to put the broken family together again. When I hid the shattered parts of myself from my sons, I wondered if Mom had done the same. Some nights I served ice cream for dinner or let my boys watch movies when they should have been in bed. I was mothering on autopilot, too consumed with my own grief to be anything other than robotic. Was this what had happened to my mother? The robot, the mythical creature?

At twenty-eight, I became a freelance writer. By then, my first husband was shacked up with his mistress, and I was a strug-gling single mom with leaky toilets or broken sinks. My mother helped by enlisting my stepdad. The years had softened his demeanor, and he'd come to appreciate the ways Mom made him feel useful. Like a proud parent, she volunteered him for handiwork whenever she could. Fixing homes was their specialty because, in her mind, it was only a physical task. It was a matter of clean sheets, fresh paint, and inspiring decor. When I told her my faucet leaked, she sent him right over to troubleshoot the pipes. But it wasn't easy to be near him, regardless of the years that had passed.

Wary, I watched him from across the room and studied the motion of his hands around a tool. When he finished the job, I double-locked the door behind him and steadied my breath before returning to the rhythm of my day, cajoling myself out of the black cloud of fear, disgust, and anger that threatened to overtake me. These emotions left me hungover, and I found my equilibrium again on a church pew. The pastor said forgiveness is a kind of freedom, and so I thought, *I forgive. I forgive.* But it was hard to look at the man's hands, to see them turning a screwdriver in my kitchen. On holidays, it felt impossible to watch him pass a napkin or a plate of bread.

Occasionally, I'd have an epiphany: *I'm no longer a helpless child. I can stop this charade.* I painstakingly rehearsed the things I might say to Mom. But on the one occasion when I'd written her a lengthy letter, she called me on the phone irate, her voice rattling like a broken window.

"If I'm such a terrible mother, maybe you'd prefer it if I were dead." Hysterics were a winning tactic. Then came the call from a family member. "Leave her alone," he'd said. "It's too much stress for your mother. Move on." *Move on.* I thought I was seeking closure, but perhaps I was clinging to the past. It was hard to know the difference.

I met Wes in 2014, long after I resigned myself to the fact that things with Mom would always be complicated. I'd been divorced for nearly a decade. My sons were teenagers by then, and I'd begun dabbling in online dating. Luckily for me, I didn't have to endure many losers before I found my winning man. After several months together, we sat on his mother Marie's sofa, beside the fireplace flanked by bookshelves and framed photos of the family. I noticed the stack of board games and the half-played checkerboard on the coffee table. The sturdy tables with wrought iron legs, salvaged from vessels once occupied by merchant marines like Wes's father. Marie served crackers and cheese and handed me a warm mug of coffee with a splash of cream. They told stories: the time Wes's dad went searching for the family dog and found himself trapped on a California mountain. He had to be rescued by helicopter. The time Wes's sister, Jackie, as a feisty teen, stole her mother's car and parked it on the beach while she partied with friends. Later, she'd found it waterlogged when the tide rolled in. When Wes said Jackie was a hellion, the room erupted with laughter.

"Remember her fender bender?" Wes said, his eyes lit with excitement. "A little *fendy bendy*, right Mom?" he mocked, air quoting the words. He turned to me and continued his story. "Mom woke me up before school and said Jackie had a little accident in my car." Marie squealed with a mix of embarrassment and delight, her hands cupping her mouth and nose as if to shield herself from the verbal blow that was on its way. "The car was mangled!" Wes howled. "My first car—a sporty Mercury Capri—and I had to drive it with a bent steering wheel. The door was caved in, and the back of the car was smashed."

The stories continued as the family went tit for tat, everyone clutching a body part—a belly or a chest—as laughter choked their words. It was electric, and time with them emboldened me. It made me crave more genuine relationships. It made me realize what family could be. *Should* be. I thought the years had shaped me for the better. Heartbreak had whittled me into womanhood like a blade against raw wood. If my twenty-something self could see my now middle-aged self, wouldn't she be impressed with the woman I'd become, the confidence I'd gained? I'd learned that physical beauty was the wrong kind of currency for love. Still, I enjoyed my feminine moments. When Wes slid his arm up my back at a restaurant or a party, I felt pride pulsing through his palm. When my son told a friend, "This is my mom," with dignity in his man-voice, we went back in time, and he was the boy with the show-and-tell truck, and I was his shiny new wheels.

I took my lunch breaks during the workweek and dialed Mom's number on my cell phone. We talked about the magazine stories I was writing.

"I interviewed a man with a tiny dog that wears sunglasses and tennis shoes. He drives miniature sports cars for charity."

"The man drives little cars?" she asked.

"No, the dog. He has a Bugatti and a Benz. He jumps right up to the wheel." We laughed. I stabbed my salad with a fork.

"Text me pictures," she said. "Oh, and did you see the pic I sent you earlier, the tiles we just put in the hallway? Aren't they gorgeous?"

Mom lives in a small house with striking blue walls, the color of Chinese pottery. She painstakingly decorates and redecorates, buys cushy throw pillows and thick designer rugs. Every few years, she and her husband start a new project. They rip out the floors, replace the granite vanities in the bathrooms, paint a room violet, or remove the shower doors in favor of something fancier, something spa-like. These are the things she speaks freely about, her meticulously feathered nest where she folds clean towels into perfect squares. She dusts the lampshades and lightbulbs. People always forget that light attracts dust, but not Mom. My mother remembers these things. She'll tell you that millions of bacterial organisms live on your shoes, and most even carry traces of feces found in animal waste, so take them off before entering the house. And, God forbid, don't put your purse on her table. It's probably been in the filthy public restroom.

I can't say I hadn't inherited Mom's brand of neurosis. I conducted my Sunday cleaning rituals by making a soapy path down the hallway in my home. I sent my men to their respective rooms while the floors were drying: Wes to his office, my nineteen-year-old son, Sym, to his bedroom, watching YouTube videos. While some women say cleaning is a chore, I considered it cathartic. I spritzed vinegar on the patio doors, and the doggy-nose prints disappeared. The backyard was a dewy shade of green, with streaks of sunlight and a tangle of swaying trees. The best way to see the world was through clean windows. I shook out the sofa pillows, folded a throw blanket into thirds, and smoothed its hem. When the tile floors shone and the bedsheets were warm and fragrant, our house became a haven. Like Mom, I found solace in uncluttered spaces, in polished surfaces and rooms that were clean and bright. When life was muddy chaos, I grabbed a mop, made a bed, and rearranged the furniture. And it felt something like control. Perhaps I was clinging to my memories of Sunday cleanings with Mom. I cherished those moments when I had her full attention because my stepdad worked that day. I relished the time without him, the warmth of our home when he was away. It felt good, like just-dried sheets and fluffy towels. I wanted to help Mom make everything cleaner, brighter. When she handed me a lambswool duster, I held it like a royal scepter and silently made a wish for more time alone with Mom. This was a perpetual wish, forever unrequited.

Now at home in the kitchen, Wes and I discussed the wedding guest list. I perched on the granite counter, swinging my legs in front of the lower cabinets. He hunched over the island with a notepad and pen, his face creased in thought. We'd already written down the family names: his mother, daughter, son-in-law, sister, brother-in-law, niece, and nephew. Aunt Rachel, uncles, siblings, and their families. Also, a few besties he'd known since grade school. We covered the "why nots" too. They were the people we hoped would come, but who weren't as close as family. Now there were the "maybes."

"How about Bill?" Wes asked, moving his pen to his mouth.

"Well, it would be a nice gesture," I said, "but he's so anti-social, and we don't want him to feel obligated to come. . . ."

We spent the next half hour deciding on distant relatives, coworkers, and people we deemed wedding worthy. But our list was incomplete. Would I invite my mother?

I called a friend, and we chatted about my wedding dilemma. Like me, Nina was a writer. She was a smart older woman with a cat named Tolstoy, a Starbucks addiction, and the propensity to say what she thought.

"The family history is haunting me," I told her. I heard her shuffling papers and imagined the messy stack on her desk beside a Paulo Coelho book and a framed photo of her daughter, the massage therapist who lived in Michigan.

"Your mom is a victim, too," she said.

My heart slammed against my chest, and then there was silence, like the still air after a crack of thunder.

"A victim?" The thought had never occurred to me. *Mom, a victim?* I had always considered her culpable because moms are supposed to protect their children. Isn't it in their DNA? I sat with the word *victim*, two hard syllables caught in my throat. I wanted to love Mom, but a part of me couldn't let her off the hook. Perhaps it was her blatant disregard for the truth that continued to trigger my pain. In the face of her denial, I felt rejected again and again.

"She's lying to herself," I said. "How does that make her a victim?"

Nina shuffled papers again as I talked it out as if I were alone on the line. "If you asked Mom about our history, she'd tell you her sunny stories. 'We used to do lots of things together—bowling, skating, eating out,'" I said in a mocking voice, fully aware of how immature I sounded. "Her memories—they're distorted versions of mine. Doesn't she see how her husband polluted everything?" My voice pitched higher, and I talked faster. "He asserted his power, went from sexual abuse to violence against me and my siblings. He pretended it was discipline. But what he did—it was more like cruelty." I thought of the time he reached into the backseat as he drove and backhanded my older sister with a force that made her head bob like a toy. An arbitrary punishment for bickering. "You can't imagine all the things I buried in my memory just to live the life she demanded. How, *how* does that make her the victim?"

Nina paused for a moment, then said in her firm, self-assured voice, "His actions affected her too. They must have. I'm not saying she deserves a pass. She fucked up. But also—she's pretty fucked up. You have to wonder how that happened when she came from a good home. Weren't your grandparents really good parents?"

"Yeah. They were." I took a deep breath, and Nina apologized for the brute force of her words.

"It's okay," I said. "You might even have a point—for once in your life."

We laughed and talked for another few minutes before I hung up and dialed my sister, Jesse. When I needed to confirm my feelings were real, she's the one I called. Jesse lived many states away and struggled with bipolar disorder. She told me she loved me and that her life was hard. Her memories were sharper than mine, more lucid and abrasive. As a result, she was quick to anger and suffered with depression, often being hospitalized until she felt stable again. I knew it wasn't healthy to rehash the past with her, but it was our thread. The thread that connected us across time and distance. She was the one who bore witness, and her validation made me feel whole. She understood and acknowledged my internal experience because it often echoed her own.

"These things happened. Didn't they?" I asked her. We grieved about the incidents Mom had forgotten, about the time our stepdad attempted to break down the bathroom door to get at me. The time he pinned Jesse to the bed and beat her with the telephone receiver, leaving a chain of purple bruises on her neck and ear. She was seventeen and eight months pregnant then, and I watched him sit on the enormous egg of her belly, her arms flailing as he rained down blows. When I ran to the phone and dialed 911, Mom picked up the extension and told the operator we were fine. "Everyone is fine."

When that didn't work, I called Aunt Rachel, and she rushed over.

"How could you allow this? You're a terrible mother!" she screamed at Mom while consoling my beaten sister. The man had retreated to their bedroom.

When I heard Jesse's voice on the line, I was her little sister, Re-Re, again. I thought of our shared bedroom in Wisconsin, the bunk bed, the pastel yellow walls, and the stuffed teddy bear I'd named Tippy. Eighteen months my senior, Jesse was smart and assertive, the leader of the sibling pack. When we were kids, she'd urged me to peel the wrapper off a stick of butter and "paint" the fireplace, and I became a little Picasso for her. Later we watched Mom take a scrub brush to the greasy bricks, crying. When Jesse convinced my younger brother, Joey, and me to take rides down the stairs in our bean bag chair, we tumbled down with glee. After countless trips, we heard the chair pop and saw the flutter of a thousand Styrofoam beads. A snowstorm on the steps in our home.

My sister had been my queen, and I followed her like an obedient little jester. When she babysat the neighborhood kids, she paid me fifty cents to ride my bike to the Stop-N-Go and buy her a pack of sunflower seeds or a Skor candy bar. For Christmas one year, she'd stashed enough money in her fuzzy pig coin purse to buy me a Jem fashion doll, based on the late 1980s cartoon we'd watched, starring female pop-culture icons who sang and played electric guitars. We'd watched the show together, and afterward we played travel agent in our bedroom, poring over magazine photos of beaches and cruise ships, destinations for our pretend clients.

On nights when the man became a tyrant, Jesse came to my defense. When I accidentally spilled my milk at the dinner table, he threw me up against the wall and swatted me like a squirming bug. In the black silence of our bedroom that night, I struggled to breathe.

"My lungs hurt," I bleated like a scared little lamb.

"I'll fucking kill him," Jesse vowed.

We talked about the first time she swallowed a handful of pills.

She was thirteen and she'd been running a curling iron brush through her long hair when it got stuck. I'd watched her tug the handle, then wind it around and around, attempting to loosen the bristles from the dark, matted strands of her hair. She became hysterical as she realized the brush only grabbed more hair when she tried to wriggle it out. Jesse's thick, wavy mane started to look like a nest. It was a summer afternoon, with just the two of us home. Jesse rushed to her closet and grabbed a hooded sweatshirt so she could cover her hair. She was sobbing and panting, and I followed her out the door as she hopped on her bicycle and rode to Grandma's house. I rode my own bike behind her, crying too. I always cried when she cried, and when she wanted to cry but was too proud to let the tears fall. I watched her pedal fiercely down the short blocks, the sun blazing overhead. My heart raced as I sped behind her. I could see the curling iron poking out beneath her hood. My sister, the horned creature.

She rode right up the grass slope and dropped her bike near Grandma's front door. I followed her inside where Grandma sat her down and began working on her tangled hair, talking softly as she convinced Jesse it would be okay. I don't know when she took the pills—perhaps after Grandma coaxed the curling iron brush from her hair. We laugh about that day now, remembering her frantic bicycle ride with the hood pulled over her horn.

"I thought I could kill myself with a handful of aspirin," she said.

"Yes. Ridiculous."

But I wondered about the deeper pain she experienced. The shame that was always just below the surface and had nothing to do with a curling iron stuck in her hair. He'd done the worst to her. But like my blue-eyed friend Erin, she didn't have the courage to tell.

At seventeen, when Jesse's boyfriend disappeared with her car, she swallowed another handful of pills, then called 911 in a panic. I picked up her infant son, my nephew, and held him against my chest as the ambulance rushed her to the hospital. She spent three days in a psychiatric ward. When Mom called to check up on her, the counselor said Jesse was troubled. I watched Mom's face sharpen in the dining room light. When her hand slapped the top of the table, I leaned in to listen to the voice on the other end. But Mom had finished talking and slammed down the phone.

"That little bitch," she said, referring to Jesse. "She told them it's all my fault. She told them horrible stories about Dad and me."

Dad. There it was again—it made my stomach go sour.

Mom pulled a cigarette from her leather case and lit it, then tossed her lighter on the table. "This is bullshit," she said.

Jesse screwed up; that was all Mom knew. She never considered how the past might have shaped her life, her mind and emotions.

Our nightmares were lost to my mother. The discrepancies that existed in our memories were maddening and confusing. They created chasms between us. When I sat down to write, I didn't think of Mom, but the stories wrote themselves. My fingers tapped the keys until my computer screen bore a tale of heartbreak. I tried organizing the facts, events, words, pieces of my mother as if she were a puzzle to be solved. I tried to find the place where we went wrong, so I could lay the words like stones and build some kind of bridge. I wrote to erect a monument, to say: *Here lies a broken daughter. Can anyone see her?*

My mother was willfully blind.

On Saturday, Wes pulled a package the size of a pair of shoes from our mailbox. I knew what it was immediately. My pulse racing, I snatched a knife out of a drawer and sliced the edges of the cardboard. There, in a neat and shiny stack, were the photo magnets of us—my arms around Wes, both of us smiling. We were barefoot in our backyard, sitting on a small wooden bench we'd dragged from our entryway. Midsummer, the trees were thick with green leaves. The sun lit up the forest behind our home. Our dog, Mia, kept circling the photographer's legs, her happy tail slapping his jeans as he aimed the camera with a squinty eye. I thought about how we laughed and scooped her up after he'd taken his shots, Wes tipping her over and rolling her in the grass. Mia's limp body yielding to the motion, then dizzy, she'd popped her head up to see the shifting yard. The kaleidoscope of her human companions.

We admired our invitations for a moment; then I placed the box on Wes's desk, and I tried to forget them. Cleaning, I thought, will do the trick. I got out a rag and a spray bottle and headed for the shower doors. My wrist ached as I made hard circles against the glass. I got out the vacuum, then slammed it around on the floor, yanking the cord from the wall when the stupid machine reached its limit.

"Why the hell do they make these cords so short?" I yelled at the empty room.

I followed up the vacuuming with dusting, and the dusting with a load of laundry. Then, with no more chores to do, I plopped down on the couch and scrolled through the menu of channels. There was a show about emergency animal care. I tried to watch it intently as a woman held up her languid pet rabbit and told the vet he'd stopped eating. After his examination, the vet concluded overgrown teeth were the problem, and the rabbit's molars needed a trim. When the show ended, I got up and walked around the house. I felt as if I were sleepwalking through the day. I couldn't stop thinking about the invitations, and the choice I'd have to make.

I decided to make a side of rice to go with our dinner. I pulled out my frying pan and slammed it down harder than I meant to. I poured a spot of oil in the pan and watched the golden liquid spread out while the heat from the stove made it pop. I thought about the wedding invitations, and the fact that I couldn't get them out of my head made my whole body flush with anger. I heard myself say out loud, "There's not a chance in hell he'll be on the guest list, and that's the only thing I know for sure."

I tossed around the idea of inviting her to the wedding—just her and not him. I made a list of pros and cons in a notebook. I scribbled my new last name on the page, trying out my Ks and practicing the new me: Rica Keenum, a woman with a husband and a whole new family. A good family. But that fact didn't make me want my own mom any less. I found the guest list on Wes's desk and grabbed a pen. I sat down and stared out the window at a woman walking her dog, feeling the weight of the pen in my hand, with both the urge and the hesitance to write Mom's name. I wanted to believe she had it in her to tell her husband she would choose her daughter this time, if only for a night. Was this too much to ask?

Chapter 3

The Question

Fed up with the ice and snow, Aunt Rachel moved to Florida from Wisconsin. Her new home had high ceilings, gray tile floors, and a screened-in lanai overlooking the backyard. Twice a week, I took my dog Mia over for a visit, and Aunt Rachel nuzzled her nose. "You're a pretty, pretty princess," she assured my drooling pit bull.

When I arrived that day, I took my usual seat across from her, and we watched our dogs sniff and bang their tails against the sofas as they vied for pats and rubs. On the car ride over, I thought about how our conversation might go, and now that I was there, I was anxious. I valued Aunt Rachel's opinion. She knew Mom better than Nina or Wes did, and could help me sort out my dilemma.

"The invitations came," I announced, twisting my ring with a nervous hand. She looked at me, smiled, then read the question on my face.

"I think you should ask her," she said. "She's your mother—of course she will go to your wedding." Her bracelets clicked together as she lowered her hands in her lap. Aunt Rachel was a well-dressed woman. She was lipstick and logic. We went silent as the news blared in the background.

Aunt Rachel had been a supervisor in the office where Mom worked. She was the one who'd taken the call from the school on that October day in 1987. She had seen Mom talking to a customer, so she told the school she was our mother, sensing the call was important. For all the ways she took care of me, Aunt Rachel could have been my mother. She nurtured us when Mom didn't. We laughed about the time I had chicken pox and cried out in the night. In the dark, she stumbled into the medicine cabinet and grabbed the pink bottle of Calamine lotion to treat my itchiness. I felt the cool medicine on my skin as she smeared it on. But the relief didn't last. I cried out for more lotion, and she came several times to apply it, groggy but dutiful. In the morning, she discovered why the Calamine had failed. The pink bottle at my bedside was Pepto Bismol.

After Aunt Rachel learned about the abuse, she begged for an answer she could understand. Why, as a child, didn't I tell her what was happening at home? I'd had so many opportunities to tell her. I explained that I lacked the vocabulary, and I feared the truth would break her heart. But it was more complicated than that. On weekend sleepovers, Aunt Rachel took me shopping and painted my fingernails fuchsia. Our weekends were for storybooks and sci-fi horror movies like *The Killer Shrews*. We huddled on the recliner in the winter with cream of mushroom soup in ceramic mugs. Flinging the blanket to the floor, she raced from our chair to the bedroom, shouting, "The Shrews are coming! The Shrews are coming!" We'd dive on the bed, scream, and giggle. Jesse loved this game, and that made me love it, too.

In the summer, we visited the park or the playground down the street. But on Sunday afternoons, it was time to go back home. I reclined in the passenger seat of her gold Mercedes Benz, watching the trees arch over the sunroof as we rumbled down the road. Sadness arched over me, too, as I counted the street signs and landmarks, the corner bars, and restaurants that marked our passage. Aunt Rachel played Motown CDs and belted out the words to her favorite group, the Temptations.

The lyrics "I know you want to leave me, but I refuse to let you go. . . ." made an ironic refrain. I didn't want to leave her, just as she didn't want to let me go. She wanted to raise me as her own, and I wanted the same. But a girl can't choose her life. If only Aunt Rachel could've turned the car around and taken me back to my little pink bedroom in her brick house on Chicago Road. I'd curl up in the twin bed with the Strawberry Shortcake bedding and ask for another story. Another movie, another hour at the playground, and another kiss goodnight.

"I could ask her for you," she suggested now. "We'll go to the wedding together. I'll even pick her up." Her face was soft, contemplative. This offer made sense to Aunt Rachel. The logistics were plausible. But I thought about how happy Mom was in her lair, surrounded by her cobalt blue walls with her husband by her side, and all her beloved decor. It was nearly impossible to pull her away to see a show, go shopping, or spend any amount of time with anyone other than her husband.

I was suddenly aware of the cold leather cradling the back of my knees.

"She won't go without him," I said to Aunt Rachel. "She won't. Why should I subject myself to another rejection from her?" I said this like a question, but it was really a statement. "Remember the last time you tried to get her out without him?" I said "him" like a growl. *Himmm.*

Aunt Rachel sighed. "Yes, I know." She watched the dogs circle the dining room table. Then, weary from the chase,

Mia hunkered down near Aunt Rachel's feet, and she rubbed the pink satin skin of her belly. "That was part of the reason I moved here. I was hoping to get her out of the house, away from him."

"That would have been nice," I replied. "But we both know she's not interested. Remember the concert you took her to last year?"

Aunt Rachel was thrilled when she'd gotten the tickets to see Landau Eugene Murphy Jr. live at a beautiful, local venue. We'd watched him win the sixth season of *America's Got Talent*, rooted for him because he had a smooth, Sinatra-like voice. But also, he had a great backstory. He'd worked as a car wash attendant in the Midwest, singing all the while. When his boss said he should be in Vegas, he got the courage to take a shot at performing.

That was Aunt Rachel's first concert after moving to Florida, and she hoped it would be one of many she could attend with her sister—Mom.

"She wouldn't even stand up," Aunt Rachel said "The whole place was on their feet, and she just sat there like she was totally bored. She couldn't wait to get home. I was so disappointed."

"Story of my life." I told her about the last time Mom and I went shopping together. Inside the home decor store, it smelled like scented candles and dried floral arrangements. We tested out armchairs and tufted sofas. We felt prickly jute rugs, and admired bohemian lamps, and whimsical chandeliers. I was in the market for a new set of throw pillows. When a sales employee approached and offered to help, Mom snapped, "We don't need any help." I was stunned, but then she told the woman a big fat lie: "I'm an interior decorator."

I stood there, confused. Then I remembered all the stories

Mom had told neighbors, friends, and even family members over the years. Her big fat lies about her happy family. On the drive home, I watched Mom check and recheck her phone for texts from her husband. I knew she was anxious to get home. I imagined the ticking in her brain like the workings of a clock: home, home, home. The outing was a rare one, and if I wanted to see Mom, it was always on her terms, and most often that meant going to her home. His home. Their home. My hands had tensed around the steering wheel as I drove, watching Mom and wishing things were different. Now Aunt Rachel wished it too.

"I still think she'll go to your wedding," she said. "It's your *wedding*." She rubbed her knee with one hand, and I found my ring and twisted it again and again as we listened to our dogs grunt and snore like a pair of drunk pigs.

I tried to imagine how a smart and capable woman like Mom could lose her identity. When did *she* become *they*? I saw her younger self in the days when she met my stepdad, our neighbor. She was a woman with three small children in a volatile marriage with my father. She often criticized other couples who spent time apart. Men who golfed with the guys on Sundays and women who had cocktails with old college friends. "Married people don't do those things," she'd said, as if marriage were a dissolution of oneself. As if commitment meant becoming an island apart from everyone and everything else—even your children. I'd spent my childhood trying to find Mom, but I could never have her without *him*.

People always asked me what I wanted to be when I grew up, as if the answer could reveal a truer picture of me, my future self. On career day at school in fourth grade, my teacher sent the students to the back of the classroom to search the encyclopedias. We pulled thick leather volumes from the shelves, the flurry of pages turning as little hands searched the world of possibilities. I knew I wanted to be a writer. But my mother? I needed a truer picture of her, an encyclopedic definition, a word I could say, spell, study. But when I asked her, she thought for a moment then shrugged "I don't know. I guess I thought I'd just marry a doctor." I wondered now if she ever imagined a life of her own, an identity of her making, an existence apart from a man.

The days passed as I considered the ways I might invite Mom to the wedding, but my gut screamed, *Bad idea!* On a weekday morning, I drove to a meditation teacher's home and parked my car. I scrambled for my notebook, digital recorder, coffee, and pens. I rechecked the address. His house was a Spanish-style structure with stucco walls and a low-pitched roof. Terracotta pots lined the walkway, and baby palm trees swayed like welcoming hands. I'd come to interview the man for a story I'd been assigned to write about meditation. He was gray-haired with wire-rimmed glasses and soft blue eyes. He invited me inside, and we sat at his dining room table. I set my recorder between us and took in the room. I saw a dimpled cushion in the center of an ornate rug, positioned near a sunlit window.

"Tell me about your history as a meditation teacher," I said. "What drew you to the practice?"

He cleared his throat. "Well, I actually started around '85 when I lost my voice. I was sick with a virus and couldn't teach high school, so I took some time off." He pushed his chair back and stood, "Pardon me, would you like a glass of water?"

"No, thank you," I said, holding up my tumbler of coffee. "I'm caffeinated."

He laughed and turned on the tap to fill his glass.

"We are 'doing' machines," he continued. "We need coffee

to fuel our lives. Multitasking is really encouraged in our culture, but what I've discovered, what I found back in '85, was that in the course of our daily routines, we sort of disappear." He sat back down and placed his glass on the table.

"So, when I was off work, no voice," he gestured toward his throat, "I think I really enjoyed the quiet—the being versus doing."

"I've toyed with meditation," I said. "I enjoyed it when I allowed myself to do it. How do you teach people to train their minds?"

"Good question," he said, making me feel like a reporter once again. I wondered if he knew how much I enjoyed this topic, how it felt incredibly timely and personally relevant. He picked up his glass for a swig. "It's about training your mind to do what you want it to do—not what it wants to do. It's really about focus. It's not like disappearing or shutting the whole world out. It's letting it all in, but not becoming attached to it."

"Not attached," I repeated. I gazed around the room and saw a Tibetan singing bowl gleaming beside a meditation cushion—a prop for relaxation.

"Would you like to try it," he said when he saw me eyeing the bowl.

"Um, yes. Sure."

He brought the bowl over and placed it in my lap.

"I use it to start each sitting session. When the mallet strikes the brass rim of the bowl, it gives a rich vibration." He swept the mallet across the rim and it made a harmonious sound. I felt the deep vibration move over me like an ocean wave.

"Your shoulders drop and your mind sinks into silence," he said. "The journey begins."

"The journey," I repeated.

We chatted some more about his trips to Hong Kong,

Thailand, and Nepal, where he trekked in the Himalayas. He told me about his visits to various temples where monks sat cross-legged in silent prayer. He talked about the tuk-tuks that zipped through the streets of Bangkok amid the chaos and busyness of the overpopulated city.

"Just so much going," he said. "But amid all this, people had an inner calmness. The difference was palpable. It was interesting—being there. And I connected so deeply with the message I heard loud and clear: detachment."

"Detachment?" I repeated it like a question. I knew the surface meaning, but I was eager to hear his take.

"The Zen Buddhist philosophy encourages us to separate ourselves from our expectations and from outcomes in general," he continued. "It's really the only way to keep our hearts safe from mental and emotional harm."

I thought of my mother instantly, of my expectations for her, of all the ways I suspected I was setting myself up for more pain and rejection. How I would attach to her response like a fly on a sticky trap. I wanted to ask this man what he thought of my situation. I wanted to scream, "How does a daughter not feel pain when her mother rejects her?" I wanted to ask this calm, spiritually-evolved man if it would be wise to invite Mom to my wedding. How could I love her while keeping my heart safe? Instead, we talked about his class a while longer, and then I went home and rolled out my yoga mat. I knelt down in child's pose, my forehead pressed to the floor. I took slow breaths. In. Out. In. Out—until my body shook and vibrated like a Tibetan singing bowl.

I was sitting in my car during my lunch break. Mom and I had just chatted as usual, and although I had every intention of announcing the wedding, I couldn't find the space to weave in the news. Or maybe it was courage I lacked.

I scrolled through online stories and found one that jarred me: *Are We New People Every Seven Years?*

There's a myth that sounds like a wonderful prospect. It says every seven years, each cell in our bodies has changed. Cells break down old bones and build new bones. Skin and hair shed, and fresh blood cells flood the body in a flux of regeneration. The body is essentially brand new in a seven-year span of time. Although the science was far more complex, I held onto this information. I scribbled it into my notebook along with the words *transformation* and *renewal*. I liked these words better than *detachment*. I sat absolutely still as I felt them sink in. Then I picked up my phone and texted my mother.

Wes and I are getting married on October 26th. You're welcome to come. Just you.

My fingers shook as I hit the send button and then waited for her response. I turned my phone over in my lap and folded my hands to keep them steady. When my phone dinged, I jumped in my seat and tapped the screen to see Mom's reply.

After everything Dad's done for you, I think it's pretty crummy that you don't want him at your wedding.

Dad. Dad. Dad. Dad. Dad. Dad. Three letters pounded me like a fist.

My thumbs pumped out a response, fueled by anger and a surge of adrenaline.

Can't you see what this is about? This is my attempt to start a new life. When will you stop forcing your husband on us?

He's driven a wedge between you and everyone you love.
Why can't you respect my feelings?

I didn't wait for her reply. I walked back to the office with legs that didn't feel like mine, a whole autonomous body. My mind heard the sound of my shoes on the concrete, step after step as my suede flats hit the ground. My face felt the heat of the sun searing my skin, the blaze of afternoon light on a day that suddenly seemed much too bright, hot, and intense. There was a low buzz in my head, the sound of anger colliding with heartbreak, emotions gone haywire in my brain. I would return to my desk, push my earbuds into my skull, and crank up the volume on my interview with a local artist. I would listen as she described the methods she used to portray the earth and its varied species with paint, colored pencil, and pen. How she captured the growth cycle of the butterfly in striking illustrations, from egg to caterpillar to chrysalis. I would shift into storytelling mode, into a world I could control.

In fourth grade, I dreamed of another mother. Ms. Shebu was a young teacher with apple cheeks and long, loose curls that fell to her waist. She wore her floral dresses cinched with a belt. Her lipstick was glossy against her pale skin, red as dewy rose petals. In the mornings, I arrived at school early to help her pass out papers, arrange the books in our classroom library, and do all the little tasks she assigned to me. I was her helper, wide-eyed and polite, and I basked in the compliments she gave. I was smart, she said, and I wondered if I had merely fooled her or if it could possibly be true. When I wrote stories, she returned them to me with comments penned in her fancy cursive script: *You have a wonderful way with words. Keep writing!*

The morning light burst in through a row of windows as I

dragged the tiny wooden chairs back to their desks. I floated across the classroom on the invisible ribbons of my teacher's perfume. Her fragrance was sweet and warm, the scent of beauty, if beauty were a thing to be bottled. I watched her stand at the chalkboard, etching the date in perfect numerals, then returning the chalk to its tray and dusting her hands against her dress. If Ms. Shebu were my mother, I would set the table for dinner every evening, fold the napkins in perfect halves, and place the forks to the left of each plate. I'd do homework without a fuss, even math. I'd write stories about girls and their mothers, about a teacher with hair like a waterfall who could transform a musty classroom into an enchanted place. A teacher who, with crimson ink, wrote my little-girl dreams on my heart without knowing the power of her words.

On the last day of fourth grade, Ms. Shebu handed me a blue spiral notebook.

"Write about your summer," she said. "Bring it back to show me in the fall."

Sometimes I did what she asked, conjuring the day's events as I lay on my bed in the evening. Other times I wrote poems. But there was a world between my words, a bottomless well of secrets I longed to tell.

When the authorities came to my school the following year, someone called me out of my classroom and led me into a room beside the school office. I saw strangers in suits with badges and briefcases. The principal, a Hispanic woman with black, cropped hair and probing eyes, sat beside them. They asked careful questions, slowly and with an intensity that made me feel important. I felt the strength of my words in that room, and when I opened my mouth, my hope-bird rose and spread her wings. I told them everything, and it was just like flying.

Later, I lay on a cot in the nurse's office, staring at the ceiling. Ms. Shebu came in, gingerly draped a blanket over me and said, "I don't know what happened, but. . . ."

And that's where the conversation faded. I have strained to hear her voice through the halls of my memory. But it has been useless. Over and over, I have attempted to finish her sentence. *She didn't know what happened, but. . . .* My beloved teacher cared enough to cover my small body, my shame, with a maternal gesture. In that drab schoolroom, her perfume bloomed like flowers at a funeral.

Chapter 4

Anorexia

As a teen, I oscillated from one emotion to the other. Me, with my purple lipstick and over-gelled hair, scowling from across the table at my mother. She'd laid out breakfast for me: fresh blueberries in a shallow bowl of milk. I dragged my spoon around the mouth of the bowl, watching the pale berries bob and splash beneath the cold metal force of my spoon.

"I hate breakfast," I told Mom. I said this every morning from the start of high school, yet every morning she called me to the table for a glass of juice and a bowl of fruit, or a slice of toast smeared with butter and cinnamon sugar. I sat at the table and narrowed my eyes until she was out of focus, a blur of a woman standing in front of the bathroom mirror with her hairspray aimed at her head. I watched the mist shoot out of the can and rain down on her long hair. She'd dyed it deep burgundy, the color of cheap wine.

It wasn't the breakfast that made me hate her. It was everything I couldn't articulate, all the ways she failed me. When she washed a carton of blueberries, placed the fruit in a bowl, and poured on a stream of cold milk, did she feel like a good mother? I didn't want her to have the pleasure of feeling that way.

Mom didn't yet know that I hated high school and never stayed a full day. I strolled through the halls carrying books, pushed through the crowds, and then headed out the heavy double doors. I walked to nearby parks with friends where we smoked cigarettes and sipped cans of Coke on old picnic benches, sang songs, and penned names on the pages of our notebooks. Names of boys and bands and people we wanted to be. Time with friends eased my loneliness, but it never really went away. I had a sense that I didn't belong, not anywhere. I wasn't at home at home, and Aunt Rachel's house was merely a retreat. School wasn't the place for a lost girl, too white to be Mexican, yet too Mexican to be white. The Latina girls wore gold nameplate necklaces that said *Jose* or *Jesus*—their boyfriends. They dated cholos who wore khakis and wife-beater shirts or flannels with T-shirts exposed. The girls called each other "chica" and "mama." And they called me that too, sometimes. But I felt like a phony in their presence, the girl with dark eyes and ethnic hair but broken Spanish and a white last name. The name of my dad who wasn't my dad. My Black friends were hood girls, and my white friends had drunk or absentee parents. They liked heavy metal, headbangers, and menthol cigarettes. Who was I? I had a clean home in a suburban neighborhood, a mom who worked hard, wore heels, and passed out lunch money the nights before school. But I longed for understanding and validation, a piece of something that seemed missing wherever I went.

When Mom finally learned about my attendance, I felt another flash of hatred for her as she stormed into my bedroom and barked like an angry dog. I was taking away her ability to feel like a mother. Undoing the morning blueberries.

When she lunged at me while I lay on my bed, I thrust my legs into her stomach and watched her stagger backward, clutching her middle. She stood frozen for a second, stricken with disbelief before coming at me again. My legs propelled out of instinct, a vehicle thrown into drive. Once again, my feet crashed into her, and she reeled, then lurched toward me again. When she tired of this game, she ran into the kitchen and retrieved the Yellow Pages. I heard it *thunk* down on the table, a brick of a book that we sometimes used to find delivery pizzas, Chinese food, or a place to repair broken jewelry. It was 1992, and the internet was a paperback tome. She frantically searched the pages, flipping here and there for the name of a mental institution, someplace to take my crazy ass. I was out of control, she said. A *fucking mental case*. But the phone book was a threat, and in a few decades I'd understand. I'd feel the same desperation as I dealt with my own troubled teen who was also in pain.

One afternoon I got drunk on too much punch made with a little of this and that. It tasted sweet and burned going down, so I drank it fast. The cold liquid turned warm in my bloodstream, and it seemed to take the weight from my limbs so that my whole body became light. When it reached my head, I was floating. A helium balloon of a girl. I wanted more floaty nights like that. But hours later, I threw up on myself while lying in bed. Too weak to lift my head, I let the vomit slide down the side of my mattress. When I had the strength, I used the vacuum cleaner to lift the mushy remnants from my bedroom carpeting. After that, the smell of vomit returned whenever anyone clicked on the vacuum, a kind of haunting of my sins.

When I decided to leave, I packed a bag like all kids do when they run away. Carefully, I chose the most precious things: books, jewelry, my favorite sweatshirt, and jeans. I had no destination . . . but I did. I imagined that wherever I went, there would be freedom, no pain or loneliness. I wouldn't have to fight for a place in the home. I would find my place else-where, the place where I belonged. It was out there, wasn't it?

I slept in a friend's closet for a few days. She kept the bi-fold doors open, so I could watch MTV from across the room. When her mother poked her head in the doorway to say goodnight or to tell her she was heading for the bar, I was out of sight. The closet was positioned beside the door, which made it impossible for her to see me without fully entering the room. Still, when I heard the door click open, I threw a blanket over my head, feeling the thrill of child games of hide-and-seek with Jesse and Joey.

On a Friday evening, my mother came to her house looking for me. She'd found me here before. But this time, she wouldn't drag me home. I heard her muffled voice on the stoop. A chill seeped into the house through the open door, the smell of win-ter blown through the spiny hands of damp tree branches. My friend's mother said she hadn't seen me but she would keep an eye out and let her know. Again, I felt the thrill of hide-and-seek. But this game soon revealed my real opponent, my stepdad. When I had been gone a week or so, he came for me in the afternoon while I sat in the park with a group of friends, chatting and sipping soda at a picnic table. I saw his car pull up near the curb. A friend confessed his adult sister who had driven us around town that afternoon had secretly called my mother.

"I'm sorry," he said. "She thought you should go home, and I couldn't stop her from calling."

I turned from his uneasy face to the car, from which the man had emerged with a cigarette between his lips, and a wry look on his face. We stood several yards apart, eyeing each other for a moment, like two cowboys in a Western film, ready to draw. I knew he wasn't there out of love or concern. My mother had sent him, and he was there to win the game. Always the hunter, I was his prey. Maybe he thought this scenario might also make him a hero, at least in Mom's eyes.

I thought about how he relished his role, how parenthood had given him a permission slip to dominate. He was in his early twenties when he met Mom, a young woman with three small kids in a toxic marriage. Possibly, he loved her. But possibly he was attracted to us as a ready-made family, to the prospect of meeting a greater need, his need for control. Possibly he was more than a man in love with a woman. He was a predator waiting to pounce.

I turned and ran in the other direction, my feet tearing through the grass with the force of a machete. I swerved around pine trees and sugar maples, not daring to look back but imagining the heat of his breath on my back, the sharp familiar feeling. The park was surrounded by homes, single-family ranches made of brick with metal awnings arching over front-facing windows. I thought about ducking behind a row of shrubs, but they were too dense and low to the ground. I spotted a station wagon parked in a driveway, and I checked the doors in a panic. Locked. I looked around and there he was—emerging from behind a house. Again, the wry look on his face. His baseball cap had blown off somewhere in the park, revealing tufts of dirty blond hair.

"You're in so much fucking trouble," he said, shaking his head. I could see a decade of hatred in his eyes, swirling like hurricane winds. He approached, snatched my arm, and forced me back to the car. We drove back home in silence as he smirked, adjusted the radio, and caught his breath.

After this, there were other games of chase. Days when he drove to my high school but found me blocks away, hanging on street corners with friends, waiting outside the Mexican grocery for fresh batches of churros. I didn't run. I just pretended I didn't see his enormous work truck idling in the street. Him sneering in the driver's seat. Perhaps I had learned that running was futile. Pretending was a better game.

The dynamics would shift when I became an adult, a wife, and then a mother. He'd no longer wield his power, so he'd become helpful, always ready with a tool and a fix. Secretly, I saw this behavior as another attempt at control, or at the very least, a means for him to prove himself. Never mind that he had damaged the family. After all, he could repair more tangible things: a car or a broken sink. Wasn't he useful? Wasn't he needed?

Time would bury our painful history, so that all the visible layers would show him being decent and mostly cordial. And though I'd sensed a monster still lurked in his shadows, I'd learn to disable my instincts. Good girls don't put up a fight, and I wanted to be good for my mother.

Sometimes, I watched my stepdad putting a piece of furniture together, tightening a screw in the afternoon light. He appeared like any man, and for a moment I felt pity for him. I didn't know much about his upbringing, only the stories he told Mom about the boys who chased him home after school. Boys with bats or fists full of rocks. In those moments, I could feel something other than disgust for him. When I saw him with hot tears on his face, mourning the loss of his brother, who'd tied a rope around his neck and ended his life, he was human. He was blood and bone, salt and tears. Just a man like any other. But those glimpses were rare in my teen years.

When summer approached, Mom planned a family trip. She and my stepdad bought a used travel van, black with an A-Team vibe. When they pulled up in the driveway with it,

I was intrigued. I walked around it, kicking the tires like a buyer inspecting a vehicle for purchase. Inside, it was decked out with interior lighting, plush seats, and captain's chairs with their own side tables. I sat down in one of the chairs and spun around, stroked the soft interior. It was cozy, I had to admit. I imagined myself reading in the chair as we rumbled down the highway, my brother, Joey, in the seat beside me, listening to music on his Walkman. Mom said we would drive to Tennessee, and I envisioned the Great Smoky Mountains. I had never seen mountains in real life.

At the dining room table, Mom sat with the wall phone pressed to her ear. She held her credit card in one hand and read a series of numbers to the hotel reservationist. I was excited about this adventure, but I didn't want to make a fuss. I stood near Mom in the dining room and listened to her make our plans while I watched the elderly neighbor outside our window. She was long and lean, a gray hippie who spent entire days rocking on her metal swing and gazing into nowhere with one hand mechanically rubbing her cats. I thought of a worn-out record, spinning endlessly on the turntable. Her days all the same, her sad life, this cat lady. I felt the hollow pit of need within me, and I was tired of filling it with rage toward my mother. This trip gave me something to look forward to, new scenery to break the monotony.

When Mom ended her call, she scribbled some notes on her pad. "The hotel has an indoor-outdoor pool," she said. This made her a very good mom. Vacations are what happy families do.

When Mom decided she would start a diet before our vacation, I liked the idea. I'd put on some weight since taking a job at a Dunkin' donut shop, and I thought I could lose ten pounds. Her husband had begun driving his semi out of town, so Mom and I joined forces. We grocery shopped for fruits and vegetables, diet sodas and herbal teas.

"Will you eat this?" Mom asked, holding up a brand of fat-free yogurt.

"Sure," I said. "How about the lemon flavor?"

This new world of diet foods and weight loss goals brought us together as a team.

"Oh, my goodness, has toothpaste always been this delicious?" I joked when brushing my teeth after a day of salads and cabbage soup.

Mom laughed. "We're going to be skinny with sparkling teeth."

One morning, I walked to a video rental store and found an array of aerobics tapes. Mom and I tried them out in the living room, wearing T-shirts, sweatpants, and sneakers.

"How the hell are you keeping up with these steps?" she asked, panting.

"It's easy," I said. "Like dancing."

I pressed the stop button on the VCR so I could show Mom the grapevine in slow motion.

"Step to the side. Now with your back leg, step again and tap." I watched her repeat my rhythm until she'd mastered the moves.

At my favorite used book store, I bought books about dieting and cooking light. Mom and I shopped for ingredients, and I baked her a low-fat coffee cake with fresh apple jelly.

"This is the best thing I ever ate," she said, licking her fork after a bite. She was proud of my cooking, my aerobic ability, and my weekly progress when I stepped on the scale. For once, I felt like my mother's daughter.

In a notebook, I recorded my calories. At fifteen, it didn't take much for me to shed five pounds in a week. I liked the feeling of accomplishing a goal. The bathroom scale obeyed, and Mom was impressed. When Mom spotted an exercise bike at a yard sale, we lugged it home. We'd been out looking for roller skates—trying to find new ways to burn calories. We placed the stationary bike on the living room carpet in front of the television, then Mom handed me a paper towel and spritzed the bike with spray cleaner. We each wiped down one end, from the dusty wheels to the handlebars. Then we took our turns riding. Mom paced herself, her body bouncing as her feet worked the pedals. Ten minutes in and she was red-faced and gasping for air. That was enough for her. I hopped on with gusto, positioned my feet on the pedals and pushed my legs. My feet snapped into a rhythm as the wheels whirled around on their base. After fifteen minutes I was breathless, and my sides ached as if I'd been kicked. Mom sat across the room with a tall glass of water and a cigarette, watching as I gave her a show like the Tour de France. From the dining room phone, she dialed her friend Sally, a blonde woman who was divorced and now married to vodka. But at least she was fun.

"You should see her go," Mom told Sally, arching her eyebrows in my direction.

Twenty minutes, then thirty. My whole body was on fire. Hot blood rushed through my veins. My chest tightened, and my legs became battering rams, fighting the pain and fatigue. At forty-five minutes, I proceeded with trembling legs. I was riding a stationary bike, but I felt myself moving forward, racing away.

Later, Sally came by, and Mom said they were dyeing their hair. Did I want to dye mine too? At the beauty supply store, we picked out a burgundy shade like the one Mom used on her hair. When we returned home, she gave me a faded T-shirt from her dresser drawer.

"Put this on," she said. "In case the dye drips."

I took the shirt happily and rushed to my bedroom to change. In the dining room, she pulled out a chair and told me to sit. Then she draped an old towel around my shoulders. She got to work with the dye, mixing the chemicals and shaking the plastic bottles as the pungent odor stung my nostrils.

"Look at this mess," she said to Sally as she raked her gloved hands through my hair. "Nappy girl," she joked. "*Sucia.*"

Although I'd long ago lost most of the Spanish I learned as a child, I liked to hear Mom speak the language. It made me feel that she was acknowledging my heritage, that she wasn't ashamed anymore. After she and my Mexican dad divorced, this wasn't the case. She'd stopped being proud of her children because we didn't look like the new white man in our home. She stopped buying barbacoa from El Rey Food Market, making chicken mole and ordering us around in Spanish—ven acá, sientate, cállate. She gave us her new husband's German last name. When I asked her what to tell the kids at school about the new name, she said, "Tell them this was always your name." What I heard was this: *Forget who you were; it's not good enough anymore.*

"Tilt your head back," she said, gently tugging my hair. She worked the color in and I listened as her plastic gloves smooshed against my dye-soaked hair and made a soothing sound, like white noise. I closed my eyes and savored her hands on my scalp. My mother's hands. And it wasn't at all like the times she clawed my head in the bathtub when I was a little girl getting my hair washed. She was impatient then, annoyed at my squirming and fussing and all the trouble of raising three kids. Dyeing my hair, she was tender.

With Mom as my friend, my new hair color, and my rapidly shrinking waist, I became obsessed with dieting. My mind was a calculator, forever counting calories. In the early mornings I stood naked on the bathroom scale, heart thumping as I waited for the cheap device to tell me how much I was worth. I pulled on my work uniform, feeling a sense of power as I cinched my apron around the narrow curve of my body. I had gone from slightly chunky to magazine-model skinny. Soon, I'd be emaciated. At the donut shop, the regular customers buried their faces in newspapers. But when I made my rounds with a pot of coffee, people nodded and smiled.

"Looking good," one man said with a wink. Everyone approved. Skinny was synonymous with love—love from Mom and the rest of the world too, even strangers. They didn't know about the notebook I used to record my calories, or that I'd drastically cut my intake because I liked to feel my stomach walls clamp shut. Food was no longer fuel. It had instead become my enemy. I stopped hanging out with school kids and instead spent all my energy on routines, tedious new habits they wouldn't understand. How would I explain to my friends that we couldn't walk to McDonald's anymore and order large fries and Cokes while we talked about boys? How could I tell them I didn't want to raid the broken vending machine at the laundromat and fill up on Doritos and Snickers bars.

There was a motor running inside me and it revved up day and night. The sound was so loud it was all I could hear. That motor drove me away from food, steered me toward the bathroom scale where I stepped on and off to see if the numbers changed. Then, I stared at myself in the mirror, a pile of bones. Mom and I played workout tapes in the living room, and later, I played them again when the house had gone quiet and she was in bed with her husband. She didn't know I was unstoppable, how I foisted my tired body into action. I had to stay thin to stay loved. I couldn't shut the motor off.

Jesse flat out refused to vacation with the rest of us. Her hatred for my stepdad had grown as she fought for her independence. They bickered daily about everything from the way she washed the dishes to the way she parked her car. This was the year before her first pregnancy. The following summer, Mom would find a pamphlet for teen mothers in Jesse's car. The baby's father was a handsome Black boy named Kenny, thin and tall, with a perfect smile and a laugh that made you laugh too. When Mom prodded Jesse to consider abortion, I wondered if she was giving the advice she wished she'd gotten when she became pregnant at seventeen. That was the beginning of a deeper rift between Jesse and Mom, and the fights would worsen until Jesse moved to a tiny rental on the gang-infested Southside with her infant son and new boyfriend, Javier, the soon-to-be father of her second child. And that year before she left, I'd watch my pregnant sister standing in front of the pantry wearing sweatpants pulled up to the knees and a T-shirt two sizes too big. She'd rip open packets of Saltine crackers and dip them in peanut butter. I'd stare at her waist-length wavy hair in the afternoon light, the way the sun turned it to beautiful auburn flames. It made me wonder why people had mistaken us for twins. In my mind, our differences were obvious. I had dark curls, stiff and shiny, greased with styling gel, and my eyes were a deep shade of brown, while Jesse's were big, and black as a starless night. She wore mascara on her lashes and Coke-can red lipstick on her perfect lips— heart-shaped like Betty Boop's. I painted my eyes with liquid liner, curving the outer edges with thick, glossy strokes. These simple makeup tricks were a part of our signature styles.

During that summer trip to Tennessee, Jesse stayed behind with friends and worked lots of shifts at a low-end restaurant.

I sat in the back of the van with my brother, Joey, and his scrawny neighborhood friend. When we stopped to gas up or grab a meal, they disappeared to smoke weed in secret, behind gas station bathrooms and rest stop pillars. I watched them emerge with eyes glazed and laughing.

"Stupid boys," I said.

I had a paperback copy of Gone With the Wind, and its sequel. I read for seven hundred miles as Mom sat in the passenger seat of the van, chattering with my stepdad, smoking cigarettes, and finding new radio stations when we drove out of range. I occasionally looked up from my book to see the mighty peaks and shards of rock that forged walls beside the road. In the early morning, I gazed at the dense fog clinging to the blazing horizon. Everything was beautifully brand new, and I had a suitcase full of size two shorts and extra small sundresses.

At the hotel, I sat by the pool where the smell of chlorine floated in the air. I wore my new bathing suit, a navy blue and white nautical one-piece with a little red anchor in the center. I'd brought my paperback, but couldn't focus on the words. Instead I watched as a little boy splashed his dad, a woman in a lounge chair peeked over her magazine, and the elderly couple at a table peeled away sections of a newspaper and passed them back and forth. I watched everyone, inventing the stories of their lives. When they sipped sodas or munched on tiny bags of chips, I counted the calories they ate. I marveled at their careless consumption of food, and I wondered if I would ever stop obsessing that way. Could I shut off the motor if I tried?

Mom had abandoned our diet and enjoyed eating thick steaks with loaded baked potatoes and greasy sandwiches at restaurants where other tourists dined. I didn't want to watch her eat steaks with her husband. It felt like an act of betrayal. We had made goals and plans together, and now she was at his side, laughing and eating, and enjoying the trip with him. I didn't want to try out the local buffets where cowboy hats and leather saddles hung in the country-themed eateries and bars. I spent most of our vacation on my own, walking the tourist strip where little shops pumped out music and neon signs blazed in the windows. I saw racks of T-shirts and shot glasses, and occasionally bought little trinkets: a coin purse, a water bottle, a beach towel that said "Gatlinburg, Tennessee." My real goal was burning calories, walking off the dry toast I ate for breakfast. There were only a few great moments when I forgot about food and calories and exercise. Mostly, I watched people eat and guessed what sizes they wore, and I wondered if anyone else dieted. If anyone else was trapped in a body with a running motor—a body that refused to rest.

When we returned home from vacation, I was eighty-eight pounds, and my hair had begun to fall out. When I lifted my head from my pillow, there were loose strands everywhere, like that of a shedding cat. My skin goose-pimpled at the slightest breeze. I was cold even with the sun on my back as I walked for miles to the mall, to the park, to the used book store where I scanned volumes of old poetry. When I looked in the mirror, I was afraid of the girl I saw. Skeleton Girl.

I read about myself in teen magazines—*Symptoms of Anorexia Nervosa: dizziness, fatigue, low body temperature, compulsive behavior, social isolation, constipation, absence of menstruation, depression, dry skin, hair loss, sensitivity to cold, slow heart rate, obsession with food and calorie counting.* I was desperate to fix my broken self.

Alone in my bedroom on a summer afternoon, I dialed Aunt Rachel's number. I'd stopped spending weekends with her, opting to be with my friends. But now it was just me, a skinny, shivering girl in her bedroom with shedding hair. When she said, "Hey, Cutie," I began to sob. I wanted to be her cutie, but I didn't feel cute anymore. I cried so hard, I couldn't speak. She asked, "What's wrong? Tell me what's wrong." But I couldn't get the words out. I couldn't tell her I was lonely and sick and afraid of starvation. I wanted to help myself, but I wanted to suffer too. Suffering was like screaming, a way to be heard. But no one was listening now, and I couldn't use my voice to speak. There was too much sorrow in my throat. She waited until my breathing slowed and the tears stopped coming so fast.

"I'm okay," I said, and hung up.

Ultimately, it was my mother who came to my aid. But not before I tried and failed to save myself. I decided if I forced the food down, then maybe I could overcome my problem. It would be like jumping into a swimming pool to get over the fear of water. I thought about how I would do it and formulated a plan one day as I worked the cash register at Dunkin'. The door dinged as new customers entered and formed a line. As they studied the racks of donuts behind the counter, the glazed, powdered, and cinnamon sweets, I rehearsed the plan in my mind.

After my shift, I folded my sugar-dusted apron into a tidy square and tucked it into my purse. I walked a few blocks to a Ponderosa restaurant. I skipped the salad bar and went straight to the dinner rolls, mashed potatoes, congealed gravy, and breaded fish sticks. I piled my plate high with all the things I hadn't eaten in months. If I could force it down, I could be normal again. If I could eat, I could heal.

I watched my fork wobble as I raised it to my lips, loaded. The first bite was slow and cautious. I felt the weight of the food on my tongue and considered spitting it into my napkin. But it was so salty and warm. The fish sticks were greasy and the potatoes were smooth. The rolls were fluffy and moist. When I swallowed, it went down hard like a giant pill, but then it got easier. Bite after bite after bite. As I crammed the food into my mouth, I thought about what I'd eat next: apple pie, bread pudding, or tiny éclairs with swirls of white frosting. But I never got that far. My stomach began cramping within minutes. All the reading on food and diets had taught me to eat slowly. One magazine article said that was the key to weight loss because it takes twenty minutes for the brain to send out signals of full-ness. But there I was, shoveling it in like a competitive eater. I held my aching stomach, looked around and saw the four o'clock crowd, seniors grabbing small plates from the buffet and piling on meatloaf, coin carrots, and brussel sprouts. Some ladled hot soup into tiny ceramic bowls. They had come for a leisurely meal. I tried to look leisurely too, but the pain came like electric shocks, lightning bolts in my abdomen. I shifted in my booth, observed my distended belly. I threw some cash on the table for the waitress, then took a deep breath and made my way toward the payphone in the front of the restaurant. I waddled like a pregnant woman, and felt like one too. I called home to ask Jesse for a ride. I don't recall what happened when she arrived in her little blue Ford Escort, but many years later she told me this story, and reminded me of all I'd forgotten. "I was so proud of you for eating that day," she said. "But then you almost died."

"I almost . . . died?"

"Yup."

When she said this, I felt my gaunt, teen self crying as I cradled my bloated gut. I saw Mom in the dining room on the corded phone, calling the nurses' hotline for advice. I heard the urgency in her voice when she said, "My daughter is sick. My daughter is anorexic." Her determination had been its own kind of medicine. She was dead set on helping her daughter get well.

The drive to the hospital was a blur. When we arrived, we passed through the sliding glass doors and found a pair of vinyl waiting room chairs where I sat, listening for my name to be called. I looked around and saw people of all ages, moms with squirming children and couples skimming copies of *Newsweek* and *People*. I imagined the ailments that had brought them in for their visits: asthma, high blood pressure, or a sprained ankle. When a petite nurse with a clipboard appeared to walk me back to the triage room, Mom and I followed her down the hall, where she motioned me onto the scale. I stepped up, fighting the urge to strip off my clothes. Even a lightweight outfit could add an extra three pounds. The woman slid the metal piece down the scale's horizontal bar, then wrote the number in my chart. My mother frowned.

"This has gotten out of hand," she told the nurse, who was child-sized with a black bun at the nape of her neck.

"It's okay," the nurse shrugged. "A young girl cannot be too skinny."

This was the wrong thing to say to a mother with an anorexic daughter. "Are you kidding me? Look at her," Mom exploded.

The nurse ignored her fury and reached for a blood pressure cuff. She slid it around my arm and tightened it, but it was far too big for my twiggy arm.

"Let me grab the pediatric cuff," she said to me, and not my angry mother.

When she returned with the smaller cuff, I felt the pressure as she squeezed the rubber bulb and pumped the cuff with air. I watched Mom eyeing the nurse, examining her as if *she* were the medical practitioner. Was this woman doing everything right? Seeing Mom's concern sent a warm flicker through my body, a rush of pride for my mother, the momma bear ready to pounce.

Now, more than two decades later when my sister rehashes the events, the emotions resurface as if stirred with a spoon. Is it possible that I could have died from a trip to Ponderosa? I search the internet for answers and learn about "refeeding syndrome," a serious and potentially fatal complication among those with anorexia nervosa. After the body adjusts to a period of starvation, it uses fat reserves and stored proteins for energy. The balance of electrolytes changes. Potassium, phosphorus, magnesium, calcium, and thiamine levels are affected. Consuming food abruptly can alter the metabolism and cause a dangerous shift in fluids and electrolytes, resulting in compromised cardiovascular status, respiratory failure, seizures, and even death.

I can't say what actually happened to me. But after that night at the hospital, Mom set me up with a dietitian, who helped me make slow, steady changes. "Let's try an apple for breakfast," the woman had said. "Start small."

Baby steps led me back to some kind of normalcy, and over time I found myself abandoning my notebooks, my diet, and my vigorous workout sessions. When I think of this now, I am in awe of Mom's resourcefulness, and the way she'd blasted the nurse the night I got sick. And then, how she'd made all the necessary calls, found an outpatient program for me, and worked out the details with the insurance company. Her contorted face upon seeing the numbers when I stepped on the scale. Torturing myself with anorexia became a way to torture her, and that was rewarding. She hadn't felt my pain when her husband molested me, but she felt it now somehow. I thought of the way a metal detector scans the terrain for buried treasures. Anorexia was a tool I'd used like a magnet to attract my mother's love.

Chapter 5

Splinters

W es's mother handed me a coffee and I cradled the mug in my palms. "Thanks, Marie."

"I know you don't say no to coffee," she said, smiling.

She sat on the opposite sofa, her face lit by the arched window that overlooked the tree-lined front yard. This was the place where Wes grew up, the house his parents spent his childhood building. Just beyond the window, a large brass bell was anchored on a weathered post, a piece of his father's history as a merchant marine. A homemade zip line was strung between trees, and a child's swing was affixed to a knotty branch. In the backyard, the acreage splayed like a rugged carpet, fat oaks forged a family of old hands that reached toward the sky. The wind whispered stories in my ears, tales of baseball games, tree house adventures, and pets who had come and gone.

On most visits, we eventually sauntered to the screen porch at the back of the house. The wind pushed in and nostalgia washed over Wes's face. His mother took a seat in a wicker chair beside us, her slippered feet propped on an ottoman. A small woman, Marie was warm and smart. Her round face was soft and dewy, like an ad for Oil of Olay. A fan of rock bands and library books, her daily walks, and volunteer work. She kept busy and was, in my mind, much younger than her actual years. A recent widow, she was prone to unexpected tears, as the rush of certain memories collided with her current reality. When this happened, we paused and waited in obedient silence, like pedestrians caught in traffic. And when the conversation moved again, Marie settled into her familiar smile. When I saw her grief-stricken face, I wondered what it meant to lose your lifelong partner, how it felt to pack your husband's socks and shirts in a box marked for donation. I wondered if she bought too much meat at the deli, still cooked for two, then remembered there's only one mouth left to feed—her own.

Wes often relayed to Marie how we met, our first date and the way I stiffed him when he reached for a hug. "I didn't know what to think of her. Her eyes were all over the room. She wouldn't look directly at me."

"I was nervous," I said, slapping his blue-jeaned thigh. "I wasn't an experienced dater like you." I stuck out my tongue, and he playfully attempted to grab it.

"It took a lot of hunting to find my diamond in the rough," he said, slipping his arm around me.

Marie found this hilarious, and she belted out an "ohhh," her voice climbing high, as it often did when she was amused.

Marie liked to hear our stories, and she often interjected with a laugh or comedic retort.

"Rica was attractive and smart, that's all I knew," Wes began, picking up the conversation again. "The way she talked and the emails she wrote. . . ."

His statement healed the doubt-wound in my soul. I didn't tell him I needed to hear this often, to remember that I *am* smart. It's a truth I was learning to grasp.

When I thought about why I believed otherwise, how

self-doubt took root in my consciousness, I heard my mother's voice. *You're so goddam stupid. Stop crying!*

Was this a memory or a scenario I'd only imagined? One day in a phone conversation I asked my sister. "Did this happen?"

She fired back without effort. "Yes! Mom always called you stupid."

"She did?"

"Yeah. Don't you remember the way she screamed at you at the table when she was helping you with your math homework? Or when you were really young and you cried? God, you were always crying. She called you 'retard.' She was really mean to you. I don't understand how you can deal with her."

As she said this, the dust of the years drifted away, and I could see the scene in perfect clarity: Mom's face and mine, the open math textbook on the dining room table. I felt my stomach drop.

I tried to understand Mom's anger, and the name-calling. Aunt Rachel had said, "Your mom was so young with three kids, and she never seemed to have a maternal instinct."

"Why then would she have three kids?" I'd asked, shaking my head in a mix of confusion and annoyance.

"Your dad wanted a boy," she said in a voice that was nearly a whisper. I thought about the birth order: two girls, then at last, a boy. I thought about my brother, who had always been the favorite, how he often got new school shoes and whatever else he wanted, so long as he pleaded hard enough. He was a master at that, at breaking down your defenses with his ruthless tin-cup beggary. When I asked why I couldn't have new shoes, Mom said flatly, "He's a boy."

I told Aunt Rachel it made sense now. It all made sense.

At home, I did something I hadn't done in a while: I ran a bath. I poured lavender salts in the warm running water, and took a book, a mug of hot orange spice tea, and a clean towel into the bathroom. I slid into the water and sank down, shut my eyes and listened to the sound of tiny bubbles popping. I left my book and my tea on the rug beside the tub, but when I saw my phone screen light up, I dried my hands on my towel and reached for it. There was an email from Aunt Rachel. I clicked on the message and read my aunt's words.

Rica, I thought I should share this memory with you. I recall exactly what I was wearing the day Grandma said hateful words to me. I was twelve and I was playing a game at the kitchen table. My brothers started complaining about me going out of turn and she came running into the kitchen. I jumped up and ran out the back door into the yard. She chased me into the alley and grabbed the back of my top and said, "Come here, you big cow." It broke my heart. . . .

I closed the email and called Aunt Rachel. We talked about the way painful memories stick harder than the rest.

"It's been sixty years," she said, "and that day is still vivid in my mind."

I told her how the things my mom said had shaped me. How cruel names could penetrate our hearts and become splinters in our psyche. I imagined my grandmother, the gentle woman who swaddled babies, rolled meatballs in the kitchen, and sang silly songs and rhymes.

"Well, it's only me from over the sea, said Barnacle Bill the Sailor," Grandma sang. "I'm old and rough and dirty and tough, said Barnacle Bill the Sailor." I'd watched her squint one eye and recite the song in a gruff sailor voice. In her face, I never saw anything but humor, warmth, and wisdom. It never occurred to me that Grandma could be rough like Barnacle Bill, could be a mother who said things with malice the way Mom had. I imagined Grandma chasing Aunt Rachel in a fury, reaching for the neck of her shirt, uttering the word that would become Aunt Rachel's splinter. "Cow," the word that would stick.

"We all say things in anger," Aunt Rachel concluded. "Terrible things that we wish we could take back."

"Yes." I said. "Terrible things."

After dinner, Wes and I sprawled out in front of a movie. Sym sat in the suede barrel chair beside me. He smirked at a social media meme on his phone, then flashed it in my direction. It was a photo of a cat that looked like his cat, and the caption said, "If I keep looking this cute, they'll keep blaming the dog."

We chuckled and then started chatting. My mind went back to the conversation with Aunt Rachel. Suddenly, I had to know if I'd said terrible things to my son that stuck in his memory. I paused the movie and asked, "Did I ever say anything really *mean* to you?"

Sym did not take a moment to think. His answer rolled at me like a grenade.

"You destroyed my Legos," he said, his dark eyes averted.

He told me he built something, a rocket or maybe a robot. He spent hours clicking each piece into place. I imagined his hands working, his glasses sliding down his little nose as he squeezed his face in concentration. He was just three when he started wearing glasses, pink-cheeked, with eyes wide behind the fishbowl of his thick lenses. I saw traces of that child hidden inside the broader bones and bristle of his nineteen-year-old face. When he was focused, afraid or engrossed in a task, I could glance at him and see my little boy in just the right light, like a holograph or a faintly twinkling star in the distance.

"I was proud of it," he said. "But when I came to show you what I made, you smashed it." His face hardened, and I watched his eyes narrow into blades.

I froze. My mind went black. "I can't remember," I stuttered. "I'm sure I did it by accident. Maybe I stumbled or knocked it over?" I tried to imagine a scenario that made better sense. "I honestly can't recall," I said.

"It happened." He stood up and headed down the hall toward his bedroom, suddenly intolerant of me. Wes clicked the movie back on, but the television screen was a jumble of faces and colors. A rainbow smudged on the wall. I felt my guilt overwhelm me as I desperately searched for the memory, the distant star of my little boy. I could not find the child with the Legos, the child with the terrible, angry mother. In my mind, I could only see his face from seconds ago, glowing behind his iPhone. The pain in his features as he told me I smashed his creation. I smashed it?

Wes picked up his glass and said he was going for a refill of iced tea. "Want something?"

I shook my head in a daze as the words replayed in my head: *I smashed it. I smashed it.* When Wes returned, he found me in tears. "I smashed it."

"Oh, no. You didn't mean it. You're a great mom," he assured me, petting my shoulder.

I wiped my wet face with my sleeve and nodded. "Okay. I know." But I didn't know. Not really. Try as I might to remember, I didn't know all the ways I'd failed my sons. All the splinters I plunged into their hearts.

I picked up my phone and started a group text with KJ and Sym. *I'm sorry for all the times I said or did mean things. I love you.*

KJ texted back within minutes: *Tempers run high sometimes, Mom. We understand. Luv u too.*

In bed, I tossed around and listened to Wes drift into sleep. I felt the warm lump of our dog near my feet and the rhythm of Wes's breathing rising and falling beside me. Our bedroom was black except for the yellow night light in the bathroom that cast warm shadows on the bathroom wall. I watched the distant light until my eyes blurred shut. My mind moving into a memory.

It was the day after my stepdad picked me up by my hair and slammed me against the wall. My head was tender. I touched the soft skin just above the nape of my neck, as if to console it. I pressed my fingers into my scalp, attempting to secure the loose hair. But it was no use. In the next few days, long dark strands would come out on my pillow, on my hairbrush, between my fingers—the pieces of me falling away. The physical parts he'd ripped from me. I'd thought about it often, how he yanked me up and smashed me against the dining room wall with a force that stopped my breath. Mom watched from behind the table, sitting over a plate of beef and potatoes, yelling, "Stop it. Stop it." More than a decade later I would watch my own small son being cornered by my first husband, his father. His round face flushed and slick with tears. I recalled how even the tears froze in place, stopped short by my little boy's fear as his father leaned in to scream at our child. Like my stepfather, he called it discipline. His monstrous presence, towering. I saw myself in the shadows, meekly pleading, "Stop it. Stop it."

But it did not stop. The images played in my mind. They shook me awake at night, haunted me in my bedroom. I reached out in the still-black room as if to push the memories away, chanting again and again, "Stop it. Stop it."

Wes was taking a shower when I opened the glass door and asked what he would like for dinner. He's not allowed to enter the bathroom when I'm showering, but he doesn't flinch when I stand there watching him lather his body with a loofah, an invention I turned him onto several years ago. At first he was skeptical, set in his ways and wondering how this frilly shower accessory could possibly be good for a man. But he used it and said, "I feel good. Do other men use these?"

"No," I joked. "They're only for supermodels and purse dogs."

A milky stream of soap slid down his backside and circled the drain.

"I'll just have a small piece of chicken," he said. "I ate a pretty late lunch." I stood there, inhaling the steam and watching the soap swirl on the shower floor, entranced.

"What?" Wes asked. "If you don't feel like cooking, I don't mind picking something up."

I was thinking, but not about takeout. "It's not that," I said, feeling my hands shake. "I invited my mom to the wedding and she blew up. She said I was out of line for not inviting . . . *him*."

Wes rubbed his arms and chest with his loofah. "Well, you knew that was coming. Don't tell me you're surprised." This was a statement, not a question. He turned back toward the showerhead, rinsed his face, then tossed his head back as the water ran down his neck.

I felt a lump in my throat, a flame in my gut. I don't know what I expected him to say, but that was not it. His nonchalance infuriated me. In an instant, I was back in elementary school, the girl who just told her mother it was true—what they said he did, all the awful things. But Mom was unfazed. I saw her in Grandma's house, she wore a blue fur coat that smelled of perfume, cigarettes, and chewing gum. I waited for her eyes to find me, but I was invisible. I was desperate to prove my case. When I said, "I swear on the Bible it's true," she looked at me with scorn.

"Don't be stupid."

Watching my husband resume his shower, I felt invisible

by his side. The word "stupid" rang in my head. My pain didn't matter to her, and now to him. I was a fool for thinking it should. A fool for inviting my mother to my wedding. Stupid, stupid girl.

In the kitchen, I took out the essential spices: garlic, sea salt, chili powder, and black pepper. I warmed the indoor grill and took two chicken tenders out of the fridge. A longtime vegetarian, I cooked separate meals every night. I stood near the humming grill with raw chicken, replaying my husband's comment in my head and resenting him for everything—for the feel of cold raw chicken in my hands, for the feel of my own raw shame. Wasn't it easy for him, the boy with the father who coached baseball, the mother who gave hugs and called to say she laid mulch in the yard around the oak, planted flowers for the wedding. "Anything else I can do, Wes? You just let me know. I love you. . . ."

A rage anthem kicked up in my head. I thought of night shifts in the healthcare industry. My coworker joked that when things got so stressful you wanted to puke, you could have a private rave in the bathroom. Flicker the lights, bang on the walls, scream until your ears popped off. Just rave yourself out with a song. I felt music pulsing, an internal clamoring riot. Alanis Morrisette's "You Oughta Know" or Pink's "So What."

I wondered if I was, at that moment, the woman who smashed her son's Legos. I plucked hot chicken off the grill and placed it on Wes's plate beside a steaming serving of broccoli. When he came into the kitchen and reached for it, he clumsily dropped it on the floor. I felt the room spin with colors, a disco ball of red fury. Wes nudged the steamed broccoli around on the tiles with his foot, attempting to form a pile. The hot stems broke and shed their flowering heads, leaving little green pieces all over the floor. I watched my husband-to-be, careless with his words, and now his food and my newly mopped floors.

I rushed into the garage and snatched the broom. I heard myself yell, "You don't respect me. You don't appreciate what I do around here." I pushed Wes aside to sweep the floor. He stood beside me looking helpless, a lost child at the mall. I yanked the plate from the counter and hurled it across the room, remembering that I was a woman who smashed things, which in turn made me want to smash more things.

Sym heard the commotion and entered the room. He and Wes exchanged a look, like two doctors groping for a sedative to dose the spastic patient. I stormed off to the bedroom.

In my five years with Wes, I could count on one hand the arguments we'd had. They were brief and mild. There was no name-calling, no aggression or fear as in my previous marriage. But today, I could not stop the anger from overtaking me. I sat on my bed and sulked. Sym approached the doorway, but did not enter.

"Are you... okay?" he asked. I felt foolish, misunderstood, every bit like an off-the-rails patient. But I defended myself. I was the only one who seemed able to do it.

"Nobody respects me. Nobody appreciates what I do," I said. But the words didn't belong to me. They were the lines my mother used while shoving laundry into the machine or slamming dishes into the cupboard. They were the words that echoed throughout my childhood, her words. I hated that they lived in me, like splinters.

Chapter 6

Dearly Beloved

S he would love to help—with the planning, the setup, and the flowers.

"Did you know I have lots of experience with dis, my friend?" Her Brazilian accent turned the word *friend* into two syllables. She gave gifts prodigiously: little mesh bags of polished rocks, turquoise beaded earrings, postcards with colorful artsy cats, or a vintage Eiffel tower. She crammed her designer handbags with flea market finds and souvenirs from trips abroad. She greeted me with a perfumed hug and her beautiful black eyes brightened when she drew out a trinket wrapped in tissue paper and tucked in the pocket of her tote.

I'd wanted to include Nadege in something, my old friend and former coworker. After I had learned I needed another pair of hands to zip my wedding dress, I invited her to the alterations shop for a fitting. We met in the parking lot on a Wednesday after work. I pulled the bundle of plastic containing the lacy heap of my dress from my car.

"Ohhh," she marveled, "you are going to be a beautiful bride. I am so happy for you and Wes." She hugged my neck and kissed the side of my face. I felt her lipstick stroke my cheek like a paintbrush.

Inside the shop, we scanned the photographs that zigzagged all over the walls: teens in sleeveless prom gowns, brides in various shades of white, kids in costumes, and men in navy or black formal wear. There were stiff smiles and loose smiles, smiles unhinged and broken open by laughter. Nadege was in awe of the photos. She took out her phone, stood back, and snapped a picture of the collage, and then another of me. Being with her was like being with a tourist or a tour guide. She took endless photos of everyday things: whimsical teacups at local diners, clouds in formations like flocks of sheep. She urged me to stop and look around. Once, on our way home from a wildlife park, she insisted I stop the car so she could roll down her window and take a shot of a mailbox that looked like a country cottage, with its shingled roof and buttercup yellow door.

I adored this about Nadege, her sense of intrigue and appreciation for everything from mailboxes to wild flowers tangled along the fence-line. She was a collector of photos and baubles, things she could share with the world. And with gratitude, she accepted every gift the world offered her too: butterflies on day-lilies or calendulas, and smiles from perfect strangers.

The seamstress greeted us and pointed to a dressing room down the hall. I imagined she thought Nadege was my mother. Her daughter was exactly my age, but she lived in another state. Sometimes a waitress looked curiously from Nadege to me, as if weighing the possibilities. *Daughter, sister, friend?* Who was I? I found myself interjecting quickly, asking about the pie or the daily special, anything to cut off the real question before it could be asked. It was hard to tell the world she's just a friend—a good friend, that's all. I preferred the fantasy of sipping coffee with my mother at our favorite diner.

The dressing room was too small for the two of us and my dress, so Nadege stood just outside the curtain, anxious, like a child waiting to pee. When it was time to zip up, I cracked the curtain open and she reached in and slowly drew my zipper up the track. I could feel her smile on the back of my neck. When I turned around, she gasped and whipped out her phone. I laughed and maneuvered down the hall as Nadege recorded the scene. The seamstress sang, "Da da da dum. . . ."

Nadege fussed, "Slow down, slow down. *Oh,* look at you. Look at you!"

We laughed until we had tears, and the seamstress picked up her measuring tape and a jar full of push pins. I felt joy and sadness in equal measure, emotions shifting in my belly, a bag of polished rocks. And I knew it was a gift to be there with Nadege, but when I saw the hands in the dressing room, the camera in the hall, the woman who was just a friend, I thought of Mom too. *My mother should be here. Why doesn't this matter to her?* I went home with a video to show Wes, the footage Nadege took. My dress would be ready to go in just a few weeks.

At work, my coworkers made a fuss about wedding planning. "So stressful," they said. People asked if I needed help, if I was holding up okay, if there was anything they could do. It's a headache, they said, to plan such a big event. This made me think I was forgetting some major detail, some difficult aspect or another. If the planning felt easy, didn't that mean I was doing it wrong? I reviewed the wedding checklist Suhaill made and consulted with Wes. We divided the tasks. I was the head decorator, the chief of ambiance. I had yards upon yards of burlap, lace, twine. I bought spray paint, hot glue sticks, mason jars by the dozen. I filled craft store bags with baby's breath, assorted hydrangeas, golden mums, and flowers with petals like silky fingers. I ordered the guest book, selected a barrel bar, designed and created centerpieces with bronze plates, satin leaves, and tiny white pumpkins. I met with Suhaill on weekends and we shared our Pinterest finds as we sipped coffee, and later, glasses of white wine.

"That's gorgeous," Suhaill remarked as we scanned photos of women with fishtail braids and wedding updos.

"Isn't it?" I said. "Let's watch some videos and see if we can recreate this style."

Wes was ever cheerful in action mode, an eager and organized groom. He made trips to a local farm in his little red pickup truck and loaded bales of hay we would use for seating during the ceremony. Night after night, he abruptly rose from his plate while we ate dinner. He rushed to jot down a question for the caterer: Should we supply the ice? He met with the liquor store owner to discuss red wine, white wine, and beer. Were mixed drinks a popular option?

"I just want everyone to have a really good time," he told me. His eyes were far away, as if he could already hear the music. . . Ed Shereen, "Thinking Out Loud" or John Legend, "All of Me." I could almost see the reflection in his eyes: the guests huddling and swaying on the dance floor. I was thrilled that he was thrilled about our big day. Also, I felt the occasional pang of guilt for thinking about Mom, the one source of drama in all of the otherwise stress-less planning.

On the day before the wedding, I had sipped three cups of coffee by the time Suhaill came over.

"How are you feeling?" she asked, several octaves higher than her normal voice.

"Good. Ready to roll!" I said, raising my coffee mug as proof.

We drove to the store for last-minute items: a few tablecloths, a dozen fat pumpkins, hair pins to secure my flowered head-piece. My dress had been hanging in Marie's closet for weeks, and we'd been making weekend trips to drop off decor. The party rental venue had assembled a thirty-by-sixty foot tent.

On the grassy plain of Marie's backyard, it looked like a pop-up story book, a fairy-tale destination. Suhaill and I unpacked our supplies in the little tool house that used to be Wes's dad's workshop. I reviewed the lists we had scrawled on paper, and the photos I saved in my phone of various display ideas. Today was the day to dress the rustic arch in vines and a sheath of fabric, to string lights from our shiplap wall where the autumn-themed sign would hang: *Falling in Love*. I arranged pumpkins like little families: big daddy beside momma and their gourd-lings. I poked garden flags in the dirt: *Welcome to our Pumpkin Patch*. When I looked around at the sweaty crew, I saw Wes's family hauling decor across the yard, hollering, "Over here?" I saw Suhaill smoothing linens over tables and stepping back to straighten the hems.

As the day blurred into evening, I watched my sons alternately working hard and hardly working, asking, "When can we order some food?"

I shook my head and thought how some things changed and other things never would. That brought comfort and an ache. And when I finally picked up my phone and saw a message from Mom, I felt that ache again: *Best wishes tomorrow. I'll be think-ing of you*, she'd texted. Best fucking wishes? This was all she had for me, her daughter. She'd be thinking of me tomorrow? I began to pace and my breathing sped up. I had the sudden urge to hurl my phone from there to Mom's house. I wanted to send it crashing through her bubble, her private planet of oblivion.

I looked again at the words, *I'll be thinking of you*. And what might she think? Would she think of the grandsons she no longer knew, the in-laws she'd never met, the groom she'd only seen twice, the dress I chose without her, the venue that was Wes's childhood home? Would she think of Aunt Rachel who would not miss my day for the world because weddings were a pretty big deal. But apparently, my stepdad was a bigger deal, just like he'd always been. I stared at my glowing phone screen, my mother's Hallmark greeting: *Best wishes.*

Suhaill rushed toward me, sweaty and panicked. "The pine cones are blowing off the centerpieces, girl. This wind. . . . What do you want to do?"

"Glue gun," I said, and we headed toward the tent and the tables. I glanced across the yard and noted the day's work. We had successfully transformed the property from sweeping acreage to a charming wedding backdrop. I took a deep breath, tossed my phone aside, and silently vowed to delete the text.

I glued on the eyelashes, blinked twice, and then pulled them off. I thought of the drunk woman Wes and I met at the karaoke bar, her head cocked, shoulders slumping as if booze were a form of gravity. I had watched her smile and chat and fall apart as the night wore on, her eyelashes coming unglued and fluttering over her droopy lids. I decided, on my wedding day, this would not be me. I grabbed the mascara instead. I applied a plum shade of lipstick and a smoky gray eyeshadow. When I was all made up, I stared at my face in Marie's bathroom mirror. This was the face of a bride.

"I'm ready," I told Suhaill, who was standing beside me with a can of hairspray, firing like it was Raid on a Florida roach. "Okay, okay, *okay*," I said, ducking away from the can.

"It's humid out there, girl," she said.

"Well, I'm not the Tin Man." We laughed, and she sprayed me one last time for good measure.

When we realized it was drizzling outside, we panicked.

"Oh, crap, crap, crap." We watched the yard from Marie's bedroom window, and Suhaill came in and out with new reports from Wes and the deejay, who were looking up local forecasts on their phones.

"The radar looks good. This should pass through soon," she said, picking up the hairspray.

"Your privileges are revoked," I said, and she shrugged and set down the can.

"Your brother is here with his family," she told me. This pushed me toward the edge of tears. Of the eighty-plus guests at our wedding, only a handful were my relatives. It wasn't hard to feel like this was a personality contest, like bodies were actually votes. I had known that my sister did her best but could not make it. That was difficult, but I understood she had work and her kids and too much going on in her life. Now, Suhaill said my brother was sitting outside the door, bouncing his baby girl on one knee. I was the sister who wrestled with him on the bedroom floor, who as a teen wanted nothing to do with his pot-smoking friends and the girls he collected like groupies. Barf. But today, I loved him beyond words, and I was grateful he traveled all the way from Hartford.

From the window, we continued to watch guests assemble out back, a crowd of spiffy spectators. I saw Wes shaking hands and giving hugs. The grass was dewy but the rain had halted. It was show time. The door opened and I saw KJ and Sym, dapper in their suits and matching bow ties. I wondered how a mother could stand on two legs when she saw her sons in full swag, when the roles shifted, and she found that although she had always held them up, it was time to lean on them instead. When their strong arms reached for mine, I forgot that I didn't have a father or a mother at my wedding. I was a mom-bride with two man-sons at my side. That was enough to steady me for the slow walk into my new life.

I heard Pachelbel's "Canon in D" as I stepped out on the grass. My heels sank into the damp earth. Every face turned toward us, and I looped my arms around my sons and gently lifted my dress as we made our way through the soggy yard. Eighty sets of eyes probing, and I felt like a spectacle, like a circus tight-rope walker. I whispered to my sons, "Well, isn't this awkward," and I chuckled because they were tense too. I felt their stiff arms tighten around mine. Wes wore a nervous smile, and I knew he was thinking, *Let's get this over with so we can start the party.* When it was time for my sons to release me, they alternately kissed my cheek. This would be the photo I'd hang in our home, the one I cherished most.

KJ paused on cue and shook Wes's hand like a father giving his daughter away. The photographer snapped more photos. I turned to Wes, and we clasped our sweaty hands. I saw our first date in his eyes, our first vacation, our first move, and every first to come. His eyes were full of promise, and this made it easy for me to follow his lead. The officiant said her part quickly, recited a poem by Helen Steiner Rice, and ran through the traditional spiel. I nodded. She stood right next to me, but I was so lost in the moment I could barely hear her voice.

It had been five years and four months since I first saw his email in my inbox. He'd asked, *What was it about me that you liked?* He wondered why I'd reviewed his dating profile, why I took an interest. But he'd been the one to search me out, and my response was purely out of curiosity. When I saw the photos of him on beaches, posing near a statue in Brazil, cheek to cheek with his daughter, leaning on his Harley, huddled with a group of golfing friends, I thought, *He's not my type.* I was so wrong. But also, I was right, because my type had previously been a man less traveled, a diehard sports fan, a movie buff whose native tongue was lies, whose anger shook the walls, whose perpetual darkness was a kind of season I'd learned to live through. I expected, accepted, and even pitied the dark side of him. I never thought his outbursts were my fault, but I believed it was my duty to repair my broken husband.

I'd been divorced for nine years when I saw the photos of Wes. I never imagined what they didn't reveal. That he would be so different in the very best ways, so safe, so stable that even after months of dating, I still waited for the old familiar darkness. But it never came. Instead there were endless summer days, motorcycle rides down country roads, tasting the breeze on our tongues. The scent of warm grass and jasmine flowers sweeping over us. My hands around Wes's waist, my hair thrashing in the wind. There were evening walks downtown, the city throbbing around us like background music. There were sticky bars and live bands. There were yoga classes in a cramped studio where the scent of eucalyptus oil swirled among the sweaty bodies. I watched Wes attempt a downward dog, his heels straining to touch the mat. When he saw me, he smiled and crumpled his nose at the ass in front of him. And we laughed. There was a couples painting class, and a canvas we destroyed with our sloppy brushstrokes. A photo with our smocks on, me with a black painted mustache, Wes with a painted-on unibrow. There were things he taught my sons: how to change a tire, how to build a credit score. There were things he taught me: how to take what I deserve, how to be fearless but also sensible. Very sensible.

I thought of the night I told Wes my secrets. We'd been dating several months and had already exchanged I love yous. We were listening to '90s rap songs, and laughing at the lyrics we'd both memorized decades ago, long before we met. "My name is

Humpty, pronounced with an Umpty. Yo ladies, oh, how I like to hump thee. . . ."

Wes called me "Sporty" then, because he liked my wild side. When I dyed my hair purple, when I wore yoga pants with psychedelic prints and leather boots with silver buckles. I impressed him on the basketball court, beat him with my three-point shot on the playground near his house. But racquetball was a different story. The first time we played, I laughed myself out of the game. I'd knocked the ball over the wall again and again, then had to fetch it, apologetically.

"So sorry. I'm really terrible at this. Sorry. Sorry," I told the man on the other side of the brick wall, who was thumping his ball expertly but had to keep stopping to lob mine back to me.

I eventually dropped my racket and found a swing set in the shade. I got on, arched my legs toward the sky, scooping up air as I rose and fell, then let my shoes drop on the ground below. High on the swing, I could see Wes still on the court, lunging at the little rubber ball, the faint pop as it hit the wall. A satisfying sound. He joined me later, sweaty and smiling, taking the swing beside me. We made a game of that too. I told him I could go higher. I could see the bubble of the whole park below, like a child looking down on a snow globe.

But that night in his bedroom, when the '90s rap ended and there was a moment of silence, I showed him a story I'd written, the story of a girl with a painful past. I wrote it just for him, because I'd wanted to finally tell him everything, but I didn't have the courage to say the words. I needed him to know I was guilty of lying by omission. I had misrepresented myself, my family, because I wanted him to think I had everything he had, that we were alike. I didn't know the rules regarding this kind of intimacy. When do you let yourself be seen, be naked? I had only ever talked about the nights I spent watching television with my "parents," shows my mom had recorded during the week and saved for Friday evenings. What I hadn't said was that I didn't have "parents"—just a mother who would make fresh coffee, set out my special mug with the green rim and the flower design, serve sourdough pretzels or ice cream sandwiches, laugh at my jokes, tell me my hair looked cute pulled back in a gold barrette. But the conditions were these: I had to pretend I had parents, to pretend that the man on the far end of the sofa was not a storm cloud in the east, a dark form floating on the fringe of my mother's love. A permanent, looming storm cloud. My sister liked to say they were a "packaged deal." You could never have Mom without her man. So I accepted him as an inevitable consequence.

When Wes read my story that night, his eyes stayed on the pages for so long. I thought about how the words had become a border, and I wondered whether he had the strength to cross over. Was it worth crossing over? Was I worth the effort?

He finished reading, took a deep breath. Shook his head slowly, the way you do when you've taken in so much information even your brain feels heavy. He said, "How does this affect you? I, I mean. . . does this affect you?"

I stared at a smudge on the white wall in his bedroom, a fingerprint from a dirty hand. Once I noticed it there, it was all I could see. Now that he'd seen my black smudge, was it all *he* could see?

When he asked, *Does this affect you?*, what I heard was, *How damaged are you?* But he never treated me like damaged goods. So we went on the way we had started. When a storm took the power out that night, we lit candles in Wes's living room and played cards on the coffee table, the rain blurring the windows and the whole world outside so that it seemed only we existed. We were the only thing real.

It felt that way now. Standing with our hands clasped under the wedding arch, the yard full of well-dressed guests was a blur. I took Wes and he took me, for better or worse, for richer or poorer, in sickness and in health. We were bride and groom. And just like that, I was Mrs. Rica Keenum, a wife in Wes's childhood backyard, with the husky oaks and my husky sons and Marie and the rest of my new in-laws. We danced our way down the aisle as Uptown Funk boomed from the deejay's speakers, and I saw Aunt Rachel and two uncles standing with the crowd. I saw my nephews, my niece, my brother, and his wife. There were phones raised and hands clapping, and the clapping continued until I felt my heartbeat in sync with the sound, my heart beating a round of applause.

After food and photographs, I slipped on a pair of flats and danced like I was on fire. I danced with my nephew, with Wes, with friends, with everyone who stepped out on the dance floor. But when the deejay played Lynyrd Skynyrd's "Simple Man," it was time to take my seat. This was the song Wes chose for Marie. He found her in the crowd and took her hand. The dance floor cleared as they moved across the floor, their faces mapped with deep, euphoric smiles. I watched them, step, step, step to the words that carried their weight: Momma, and love.

My nephew approached and said I should have a special dance too. "Want to go next?" he asked. I didn't. I wanted the real thing or nothing at all.

"It's okay," I said, my eyes still focused on Wes and Marie. I pulled my nephew's arm, and he sank down into the chair beside me. Together, we watched the dance floor as the photographer snapped photos of the smiling mother and son.

Marie appointed us a bridal suite, her bedroom with fresh sheets and fluffy new towels for the bride and groom. Wes and I were danced out, laughed out, and partied out. We collapsed into bed after midnight and drifted into a coma-like sleep. I woke up early the next day, wearing my "Wifey" T-shirt. In the living room, I found Wes wearing his matching "Hubby" shirt on the sofa across from Marie.

"Well, there she is," Marie said. I smoothed back a rumple of hair and took a seat next to her.

"How about opening gifts?" She handed me a notepad and we began making the customary thank-you list for engraved picture frames, plant pots, vases, and photo albums with gold lettering. The cards made us laugh or smile, say *very nice* or *so sweet*. Our invitations discouraged gifts, but we appreciated the pile of goodies before us. When everything had been opened and the floor was strewn with gift wrap and tissue paper, Marie stared at me for a long minute, then abruptly took my hand.

"Family can be complicated," she said, and her eyes were sad little moons. "But you are our family now, and we love you."

Chapter 7

Lionel Ritchie and My Father

I was about twenty-three, and a married young mother, when he came back in my life. "I found Dad," my sister had said. Did I want to meet him? I did, because I could learn all the secrets of myself, and I could bring that information to my children.

"Our ancestors come from the Indigenous Americas-Mexico region, from the southwestern United States south to the border of Guatemala—a tribe of fierce warriors and keen survivors who took pride in their ceremonial centers," I would tell my sons. I'd gleaned this information from Dad's Ancestry account, but there were things I learned firsthand too.

Dad was handsome, charming, and outgoing. When he talked, his hands swept into his story, like a maestro conducting the orchestra. Slender, brown hands, and I thought, *those are my hands*. In the passenger seat of my car, I watched his body and noted the way it moved like my brother's. I searched for signs of myself in him, and I found them easily. He liked poetry, although he wrote his lines in prison. I didn't ask what that was like. I was too distracted by his confidence. There he was, inches from me, telling stories about his life, with sweeping hands and robust laughter. I could see why my mother had fallen for him, his smooth black hair and easy smile. When he told me about my mother, he didn't peer into the distance like a person in pursuit of memories. His words came fast and freely, sending little earthquakes up my spine. He was finally here, and I could ask him anything. Everything. It didn't pain him to talk about Mom, which was the opposite of how she seemed to feel.

"She was something," he said, with a head shake and a smile. "Tough." They met on the playground, he told me. "She was the only white girl in the school, but she stood up for herself. They ganged up on her one day," he pounded his fist into his palm. "We were on the playground and a group of girls came asking for cigarettes. Your mom said she didn't have any, but they knew she did." He looked at me then, as if we were climbing to the height of his story together. His eyes said, *Keep up, kid. You don't want to miss this.* "She smashed one girl's head into the other's, and they didn't know what to do. Your mother, man. . . ." He shook his head again.

I thought of how I'd battled with her as a teen. How mid-argument, she would grab my arm from behind and pull it up my back until I fell to my knees and begged for mercy. "You're so weak," she'd laugh as I squirmed. Dad was right. Mom *was* tough, but in a lot of ways, she wasn't.

Dad said she was smart, so smart. Always paying attention. "She learned Spanish all on her own. She didn't want me saying things she couldn't understand."

I pictured Mom leaning over beginner Spanish textbooks in the library, then listening intently as my dad and his family spoke the words she was learning. I could see her pretty young face studying their accents, inflection, and tone, until she could hold a conversation, could turn to my dad and say, "Sé lo que dijiste." I know what you said.

By the time I was a little girl, Mom was hurling Spanish curse bombs at the jerk who cut her off in traffic. "Estúpido. Pendejo." She ordered tacos and fresh chicharrones from the little brown woman at the Mexican grocery. At work, she was asked to translate when callers could only speak Spanish. All this from a self-taught white girl who picked up the language just to keep my dad from his secrets. And for that, he was proud.

This was the difference between them. Dad had fond memories of her while Mom had hated him for most of my life, and had worked so hard to remove every trace of him, like a stain on the rug in our home. The few things she ever said about him came out sharp, from a twisted mouth.

"He threw me down the steps when I was pregnant with you. He didn't want another daughter, a slut."

She said my dad thought females, even girls, were sluts. I didn't believe her when she said this. Nor when she told me his family was dirty, a bunch of cockroaches. I wondered if dismissing her story was a kind of payback for all the times she rejected mine. What I heard were her insults and scorn. Her stories were more about her hatred than his abuse. The way her lips pinched and eyes hardened into bullets. I could see her disgust for my father, how she hoped I'd share it too. The way I always hoped she would share my feelings about my stepfather, my disgust for the things he'd done. How did Mom feel when I turned her anger around on her, the way she'd turned my pain on me? I didn't set out to defend my dad, but I felt that her insults were somehow aimed at me. If Dad were a cockroach, wasn't I a cockroach, too?

No one ever talked about Dad. Mom made sure of that. But on rare occasions when I could arouse a few words from my grandparents, they only said, "We always liked your dad. He was a likable guy," but all that really told me was that he could make an impression. Later, I learned my grandparents had forced the marriage, because Mom was pregnant and they believed it was the right thing to do.

I sensed resentment when Mom talked about her upbringing. "Grandma knew nothing about the real world. She never even wrote a check." A busy housewife and mother of seven kids, my grandmother could make homemade barley soup and recite eighteenth-century poetry. She could sing songs in Latin and tell you about wildlife in Africa, but according to Mom, she was clueless.

"My parents were old by the time I was born," Mom griped. "They didn't know the neighborhood had gone to crap and my high school was dangerous. I couldn't tell them anything. If I would have told them half the stuff," Mom's voice trailed off. "Are you kidding?"

It was the only complaint Mom could muster, because weren't my grandparents storybook material? Happy, neighborly, parental? They had always lived up the street or around the block from us, moving to a smaller home in our neighborhood where they could babysit and leave their doors open for the constant flux of kid-traffic. They kept the cartoons on and the fridge well stocked with pudding pops and cans of root beer soda.

They were characters—Grandpa with his trench coats, fedoras, and baseball caps. In summer, he smuggled candy bars and Little Debbie snack cakes into the theaters. Why pay concession prices? When the movies ended, we played the gas station game, which was more like a shopping trip when Grandpa gave each kid a crumpled dollar. We hurtled into the store and picked through all the options: silly putty eggs, plastic water guns, little Golden Books, and watermelon bubble gum or packs of Now and Later candy.

Sometimes we followed up our trips with lunch at McDonald's, where Grandpa made a spectacle of himself by loading his pockets with stacks of napkins, ketchup packets, and straws for at-home use. Back then, you could get complimentary miniature ice cream cones, and Grandpa didn't mind bringing fists full back to our booth. The cashiers chuckled as he balanced them in his hands, whistling a tune. This was how he navigated the neighborhood—whistling, chattering, humming. A retired mailman with friends on every street. He'd taken the job after returning from the Army, requesting a route in my grandmother's neighborhood. They'd known each other since elementary school.

"He used to put snow in my hat," Grandma told me, and that was proof he had loved her even then.

Like my parents, my grandparents were opposites in every way. Grandma had gone to finishing school and grown up in a well-to-do household. Her family owned a piano manufacturing company that produced ten thousand pianos every year—upright pianos, grands, and player pianos. In contrast, Grandpa's family used wooden crates for furniture and fled from their landlords at night, moving from one shoddy rental to the next during his childhood. Once married, Grandpa worked two jobs and hoarded newspapers and restaurant condiments, and Grandma wore red lipstick at all times. It was who they were, and together, they were content. They raised seven children, and only the youngest gave them hell—my mom.

In my childhood home, there was a constant storm of chaos. With three kids by age twenty, Mom worked long days at the phone company. She scrubbed our little house until it smelled like lemon cleaner, and the dishes were never dirty. My father stumbled through the door, drunk and angry. He yelled "andale," as he spanked the stairs, our cue to leave the room. My siblings and I raced to our bedroom and listened to the muffled cursing, the slamming of bodies in a house, the sound of fury, of a marriage that was more like a nightmare. Jesse, Joey, and I comforted each other. We slept in the same large bed, scratched each other's backs at night, and fought about who would get stuck with the pillow with the brown stain that looked like caca. We made silly jokes about men with dog faces and women with big chi-chi's. We called each other gordo and feo, fat and ugly. We giggled until we fell asleep in the warm bed together, huddled up like a litter of kittens in a cardboard box. Meanwhile, Mom plotted her escape.

The man who lived across the street was charismatic, but also rough around the edges. A white man with tattooed arms and dark blond hair that he finger-combed as a lit cig-arette dangled from his lower lip. He seemed the opposite of my father, who was taller with thick black hair and skin like the bronze of autumn. The man had a long-haired cat named Smokey, a blonde girlfriend named Julie, and an upstairs rental with creaky steps. He was fun because he seemed to enjoy chil-dren more than most adults did. He liked to chase, tickle, and poke my siblings and me. We liked it, and we liked him, and we didn't know just how much he liked us too. And how fun could become fear. That man was my soon-to-be stepdad.

I must have been around five on the night we left Dad. We sped off in Mom's rusty station wagon. I was too young to know what it meant to leave my father, that soon he'd leave us too. Visits would be few, and then they would stop altogether. Mom would say the man who tickled us was my dad now. But summers darkened my skin a curious shade of brown. People asked about my ethnicity, and Mom said it was none of their business. Instinctively, I felt shame. My mother stopped speaking Spanish, and I knew there were parts of myself I'd now have to hide. I began wishing I were a blue-eyed girl and pretending my name was Stephanie.

Mom took us to the courthouse on a rainy day. We cowered near the building and she took a long drag on her cigarette before saying, "You're getting a new last name." What she didn't say was how much more that really meant. How she would erase my ethnic identity and replace it with that of her husband's— whom I was only allowed to call "Dad." He wasn't our stepdad, she said. He was our brand new father. When I think of this now, I want to believe Mom was doing what she thought was best. Maybe leaving my dad was courageous, removing her children from a household of broken lamps and late-night fights. Of blackeyes, booze, and blame. They were young, willful, and probably incompatible. But what came after was far worse for me and my siblings, and where was Mom's courage then?

"Do you remember when we left?" I asked my sister on the telephone. She said Mom and our new dad had rented a place on the southwest side.

"But we didn't have the keys yet, so we slept in the basement until we could meet with the landlord the next day. I had to go to my first day of school from there."

When she said *the basement*, I remembered the place. A mattress on the cement floor. Van Halen on the radio singing, "Jump. Might as well jump."

We had indeed taken a leap, but that didn't occur to me then. I simply enjoyed the song, thrusting my little body up, again and again on the mattress. The song pumped in my ears. There was no more Julie or Smokey the cat, and I can't remember feeling sad about leaving my father. How could I know the future, what it would be like to have a new home, a new name, and our neighbor for a dad? How could I know there'd be a day when the tickling became touching?

I had a few happy memories of Dad, my real father. Or maybe I'd confused us with a movie. We were at the park, spread out on a blanket under a tree. Dad lifted two corners of the blanket and Mom followed his lead. They swung it, side to side like a hammock in the breeze. I was inside with my siblings, giggling and peeking out of the mouth of the blanket. I watched the tops of the trees and the world swish by as we tumbled like a sack of laundry.

My sister said, "Yes, we were there. We took a trip to Cave of the Mounds that day, and we pulled over to the side of the road for a picnic. Mom and Pa were together then. Mom packed us all tuna fish sandwiches. She'd cut onions into huge chunks and I whined about the stupid onions." My sister said she wanted to turn the years back. She'd gladly eat the onions this time. "I went for a ride today," she said. "Drove by the old neighborhood, and it felt like home, like I could just walk right into Grandma's house. My heart was singing."

We talked about the visitation after the divorce. Dad picked us up, maybe every weekend, or maybe once a month. We made our rounds near the home where we used to live. There were corner stores and bars, fried chicken restaurants and drive-through burger joints. There was a three-legged dog named Sargent, and a red convertible with white interior. There was an alley with a smoking grill, a yard full of kids and patchy grass, and a man on a wobbly kitchen chair swigging beer. A car radio played a song I'd never heard, and Dad's laughter rose above the chorus.

In In the early morning, my Spanish-speaking grandma fried tortillas on the stove. The house smelled like corn and hot grease, and I stared at a velvet sombrero on the wall. It's sequin threads looked like spun gold. Lionel Richie sang, "You are the sun. You are the rain. . . ."

I didn't know how the song would make me feel in a decade or two. I didn't know that day would be one of my last childhood visits with Dad, that on my twenty-fifth birthday, my first husband would hand me a Lionel Richie CD. I'd squeal, "You remembered," and on nights when he didn't come home, when I felt the loss of everything, the flame and the heat of families burning down, I'd play my songs and I'd be the girl on a visit with her dad, in the sunlit room with the twinkling sombrero and the smell of tortillas. The girl who had yet to be touched, broken, betrayed. I'd dream that one day I could be a blue-eyed Stephanie married to my own Lionel Richie. Like the lyrics from the song, I would be someone's sun and rain.

Chapter 8

Honeymoon Mishaps

It was our first cruise, and we were excited. We had sandals, sunglasses, passports, and outfits for leisure and sport. Our suitcases were round as full bellies. "Jamaica here we come," I said, as we hoisted the bags into the truck bed. It was a four-hour drive to the port, but Wes insisted we leave six hours in advance.

"It's like flying," he said. "You have to arrive early."

I rolled my eyes and smirked as he shuffled our itineraries and printed copies of excursions. Wes had a folder, sticky note, or spreadsheet for everything. I'd come to appreciate his organizational habits, and his quirks make me feel safe. I thought of him like a rolodex or computer file, but with muscles and a motorcycle.

We were amped up, belting out the Sheryl Crow song "If It Makes You Happy." This was our 90s tour, and I told Wes we'd cover all the chart toppers while we sped to the port in his Toyota Tacoma. The truck belonged to his father, but Wes bought it from his mother when he'd died. I thought it made Wes happy to put his dad's truck to good use. It had low mileage, was perfect for the daily commute, and gave our dog Mia the great joy of riding between us on weekend outings, her tongue flapping in the breeze.

An hour into the drive, the road got bumpy, and the truck seemed agitated. I watched Wes's hands tighten around the steering wheel as it shook and spasmed.

"Shit," we said in unison. We were wobbling now, and Wes veered into the right lane so we could coast toward the exit. I examined his face for the plan. A taut lip told me he was thinking.

"We've got time," he said, patting my leg and smiling. On the side of the road, he shut off the engine and got out of the truck. I watched him circle the vehicle, then disappear beneath it. "We have a flat," he announced.

I rolled down my window and asked if he needed help. No answer. I got out and found him tussling with the rusty bolts on the deflated rear tire. He looked at me with a sweat-slick face. I couldn't see his eyes behind the knock-off designer sunglasses I'd bought him last year.

"Plan B," he said. "I gave it a hell of an effort." He hopped back in the driver's seat and we hobbled for a while in silence, his lips going rigid again. Then, like manna from heaven, a dingy roadside sign appeared: Big D's Tire and Auto.

"Hey Big D," I whooped, and Wes followed the gravel driveway to a lot that looked like a graveyard for semi-trucks. We parked beneath a large sagging carport and Wes got out to chat with a greasy uniformed man. He was lanky and bearded, and I watched him nod his head as Wes explained our dilemma. It's going to take some special tools, the man discovered. It's a challenge, but he's up to the task.

From the passenger's seat, I watched him twist his beard for a moment, then disappear into the open garage. I saw proof of other mechanics, a pair of legs beneath a jacked-up car and the tattered soles of workboots. When the bearded man appeared again, he gripped a cutting blade in one hand. With his fight face on, he went to war with our rusted bolt and chain. I watched from inside the truck as Wes stood beside the man with the tools. I couldn't quite see what he was doing, but I heard the pounding and grunting. It went on for several minutes then stopped and started again. More men appeared to watch the event like an outdoor sport. More grunting, and now there was a bit of cheering too. The man finally managed to free the spare tire. He slammed the tool down on the cement, and raised his hands as the ting of metal on gravel made a victorious sound.

"It ain't good," he said, holding up the dusty rubber donut. "But it might get you where you're going if you're careful."

Wes agreed, pulled a wad of money from his wallet and shook the man's hand. The man refused the cash, but Wes insisted and slid the bills into his palm.

With our spare secured, we hit the highway once more. "On the road again," we sang as we headed for the port. Wes recalculated the plan, adjusting the timeline: Fort Lauderdale, check in, cruise card, drop luggage, head to the bar for a drink. I nodded, turned up the radio and watched the traffic in the left lane rumble past us. We were taking it easy, driving a conservative 60 mph. But thanks to Wes's ultra-planning, we were still on track. We drove ten, twenty, fifty miles, and then it happened—something snapped beneath the truck and threw us into a zigzag. It felt like we were driving on spikes.

"Again, really?" I couldn't believe our luck. "Two flats. Two?" I was outraged, searching for the candid camera.

Wes took a deep breath and belted out a few curse words. With the truck in park on the shoulder of the road, we got out to inspect the damage. The sun and heat were intense and I was offended by the speed at which the traffic ripped past us. I imagined my body on the hood of a Volkswagen, bobbing like a crash test dummy. Wes leaned over to get a closer look at the damage. He shook his head in disgust. The tire was shredded, a sad, curl of rubber, thin as a potato peel. Wes's face was red and shiny. The color of a stop sign. We'd both had enough. I kicked the stupid tire and then kicked it again. Wes wiped his brow with his forearm, checked his watch, and took off running down the shoulder of the road.

"Where are you going?" I hollered, but he was either not listening or unable to hear above the heavy metal concert of highway traffic. He stopped, whipped out his arm, and flipped up his thumb. His thumb! I could not believe my man. I turned and kicked the tire again for good measure. Wes has gone mad. My sensible, spreadsheet-for-a-brain man was now a sweaty, hitchhiking vagrant. I stormed over to him and with every passing car, the wind slapped us like the tail of an animal. My hair fluttered up at my face.

"This is a terrible idea," I yelled. I am not hitching a ride with a stranger. You don't know who's out here—another Ted Bundy, or maybe Jack the Ripper. . . ."

Wes did not respond. I watched the road and no one seemed to notice my insane husband, who was sweaty and poised with one foot on the highway and the other on the gravely shoulder. An array of cars, semis, and SUVs rushed past, oblivious to his silly little thumb that pointed toward the sky. Every second that ticked by pushed us farther from the honeymoon ship. Still, it was useless to stand there with nothing but a hopeless thumb. I turned away from the road and began walking back to the safety and silence of the broken-down truck, which sat slumped to one side like a sleeping school boy.

Desperate, I climbed inside the truck and slammed the door to muffle the road noise. Maybe I could find a local cab. Googling my options, I called taxi cab company after taxi cab company, only to discover we were too far away. We were two stuck newlyweds on the side of the highway, and nobody gave a damn. Then I decided to give the Uber app a whirl. I hit the download button and waited for the app to load. Shit, I had to register. Of course. As I tapped in my info with racing thumbs, I thought, *This is how you use your thumbs in a crisis, old man.* But Wes was still working the highway like a dedicated street walker.

"You don't have the legs," I said to the empty truck. I heard the occasional horn honking, probably a carload of teens thinking he should spring for an Uber. Now there was an idea.

When my account was ready, I found a nearby driver and requested a ride. Bingo! She was on her way, twenty-eight minutes out—Sandra in a black Kia Optima. I flew from the truck and rushed down the shoulder of the road, yelling, "We have a ride! We have a ride!"

I gave her directions to meet us near the exit sign, since the truck would be hard to find. We lugged our bags down the hill and stood on a patch of grass. Wes checked his watch. "We could actually make it," he said, smiling.

But before Sandra pulled up, a police officer rolled beside us. His window slid down and I saw a pair of mirrored sunglasses and a sharp, clean-shaven chin. He was not the friendly neighborhood officer handing out baseball cards. "You can't be here," he snapped.

Wes began to explain our dilemma, but Robocop was not having it. He shook his head while Wes grew frustrated and eventually stopped talking.

"Go back and sit in your truck" the officer said.

Wes grunted. I felt the urge to slap the Top Gun sunglasses off Officer Pompous's face, to tell him what we'd been through and where we were headed. I wanted to say, "Back off. At least we're not hitchhiking . . . anymore." But instead I repeated what Wes said, that we're waiting for our Uber ride. Sandra was on her way in her black Kia Optima, and she would miss us if we walked away. The officer pointed to the truck and his window went up. He had better things to do than argue with the sweaty couple on the side of the highway.

Wes and I stormed up the hill and back to the spot where the truck sat like a busted toy beside the blur of traffic. *Will she spot us and be able to stop?* I opened the Uber app on my phone, thinking I could type her a message: Change of plans, meet us behind the exit sign. But I saw it was too late. She'd already veered off the highway. She just missed us.

No. No. No! I was frantic, begging. *Please come back. Just swing back around and drive a tad farther. You'll see us if you look for the truck. The little red truck on the side of the road. We're waiting here with our luggage. We're hot and thirsty and please, this is our honeymoon. . . .*

Sandra said she'd loop back around. Sandra the saint. When she pulled up a short while later, we were as giddy as two kids approaching the ice cream truck. "Thank you. Gracias. Thank you," we said as we crammed our bags into her car.

We did 80 mph all the way to the port, weaving in and out of traffic. Sandra was serious about this. She was a Spanish-speaking woman with shiny black hair and dark eyes that expertly assessed the road ahead. She swerved between lanes, choosing the fastest options. I had the feeling she was rooting for us, that she would take pleasure in telling a friend about the honeymooning couple she rescued today. *They were a mess when I found them. Desgraciado.*

Wes dialed the travel agent, left messages, urgent messages. "Contact the ship. We're late, but we're on our way." He called customer service numbers, explained our dilemma, then turned to Sandra. "How long?" She checked her phone screen, which displayed the map, then offered the ETA. "Eighteen minutes," she said.

"Eighteen minutes," Wes repeated to someone on the other end. "We'll be there in just eighteen minutes."

I thought of all the things you can do or not do in eighteen minutes. You can take a hot shower, dry off, and choose an outfit. You *can't* watch a whole sitcom or make a pot of rice, but you can heat up the air fryer and roast a batch of seasoned potatoes. If you cut them thin, that is. Eighteen minutes could be a lot of time if you're on your feet in a stiff cruise ship uniform, waiting for a pair of late newlyweds. But if you take out your cell phone, watch a few videos of little cats slapping big dogs, it's not so bad. Eighteen minutes is just eighteen minutes. In the back seat of Sandra's car, I tapped my feet and sent subliminal messages to the cruise ship workers waiting at the port. Seventeen minutes. . . .

When we finally arrived, we saw the ship, a massive white vessel in shallow water. Sandra wished us well and we thanked her before running off with our luggage.

The gate was locked. Wes slapped the metal fencing and yelled to the boat, "Let us on. Let us on." We watched the passengers mingle on decks. They were dollhouse people, with tank tops and tiny smiles, toasting the start of their adventure. They moved along the decks, oblivious to the fools banging on the locked gate below. Wes continued to call out, rattling the gate with his fists. I felt like a popped balloon. I looked away, not wanting to see the couples in their sun hats and shorts, clinking wine glasses and snapping selfies on the deck, selfie-ing on our honeymoon ship.

Why were we on the wrong side of the fence when my husband did everything right? He printed our itineraries, packed our passports, and created a folder and a timeline. He rushed me out the door, lectured me on the importance of planning ahead, and yet there we were two imbeciles dragging their luggage on the concrete while the ship gleamed in the distance on a metallic blue sheet of water.

I was suddenly overwhelmed by it all: the shredded tires, the freeway scramble, the high-speed Uber ride. The afternoon heat was pushing down on me like a hot hand, and I was frustrated, hungry, exhausted, sweaty, and in a state of shock. This was my honeymoon and I stood on the sidewalk with a dying cell phone, a hysterical husband, and no place to go. The cruise ship bobbed on the water, and I thought of the air conditioning, endless buffets, sun decks and cocktails with wedges of fruit and paper umbrellas. Then came the waterworks. It started with a single tear and before I could catch my breath, I was heaving like a wounded animal.

Wes rushed over, rubbed my shoulders. "We're going to make this right. *I'm* going to make this right." His eyes became liquid glass, a tranquil shade of green. A part of me felt ashamed for the guilt I'd heaped on him, but I knew that my tears had transformed him too—from the frenzied beggar to the man with a plan. He settled into composure, his hands firm on my shoulders. "I'm going to fix this, babe."

A uniformed man with a walkie talkie came along and asked us our names. Wes opened his file and showed him our reservation documents. He told our story quickly, emphasizing the most ridiculous part, "Two flat tires. Two!"

The man paused, then radioed another man, then a woman. They talked for a moment then sent a few more employees our way. They discussed regulations, guidelines, the Department of Homeland Security and various clearance measures. I watched the woman's stern face, her gray hair like a sponge wet with sweat. Her face like a lumpy potato. She was all business, a type-A I could tell by her wire-hanger posture.

The suits didn't bother whispering because there were no secrets. The rules were the rules.

"No one boards the ship now. No one," said another firm woman with silver-gray streaks in her braided black hair.

Wes appealed to them, talking with his gentle hands and sensible tone. They nodded, flipped through clip boards and lists and talked about the best approach. I tuned it all out as I watched the water, the boat, the sun like a bright yellow smile. I thought of the ugly 90s T-shirts with the "don't worry, be happy" face. Finally, the staff reached a verdict: We're ten minutes late, and the best they could do was allow us to meet the ship in Jamaica. We would have to book a flight, provide the cruise lines with our flight information and wait for the email stating we'd been approved to board when the ship embarked again. But first, we would Uber our way to a hotel and arrange for a tow truck to rescue the Toyota from the highway.

By evening, we were kicking off our shoes in Fort Lauderdale and wading in a hotel swimming pool. The water was silky and cool, and I slid down, shoulders deep. I found Wes on the ledge, and I wrapped my arms around him. We stared at the moon. It looked like a crystal ball, moody and bright.

"Tell me what the future holds," I whispered. "What will day two of the honeymoon bring?" With the warm breeze filling our lungs, we sat in silence for a while and exhaled the stress of the day. We had the whole pool to ourselves, except for a stray cat meandering among patio chairs. I saw his eyes glowing, heard the night wind ruffling the leaves of shrubs and trees.

"This isn't so bad," I said.

Wes made little circles on my back with his palms. His hands were rugged and warm, and I could feel the cool metal of his wedding band. "Let's see," I said, reaching over and yanking the band loose from his hand. I held it up to the moon, where it sparkled.

"Think we'll stay married through the honeymoon?" I joked.

We laughed.

"Well, today was some kind of test," Wes said, shaking his head. I slid his ring back on his hand and we laughed again. The cat scrambled from his belly to his feet and slipped through the iron gate.

"I just thought of something," I snorted. "We literally missed the boat. But hey, we're making a really great story."

When we finally made it to Jamaica, we stepped off the plane and hailed a van to meet the cruise ship at the port, a rough and jarring ride through the mountains. Our driver described with exuberant Jamaican-ease the landscape that jutted up around us on narrow, winding roads. There were paint-chipped roadside shanties with jagged roofs and clotheslines strung with colorful wares: dresses, headscarves and beach bags for sale. We zipped past motorbikes, and dented vans, and the Hummingbird Bar, which was more like a hut on a patch of cracked cement, with a curvy Black woman and palm trees painted cartoonishly next to the door. Tourism and shipping are Kingston's major industries, the driver told us as we swept past a seaport and various industrial buildings with rusty rails and climbing metal stairways. Behind these grimy structures was an impossibly blue sky laced with clouds. The mountains loomed in the distance. Some were green and dotted with trees, and others were dusty peaks, gray as a distant memory. Wes and I had our phones out, snapping pictures in a state of excitement. Our driver was proud to point and chat. He talked about curried goat and jerk chicken, botanical gardens, and banana rum. Wes and I bounced around in the back of the van, cameras aimed out the window. We drove for over an hour until we saw the port at last.

Our driver unloaded our suitcases and sent us away with bottles of water. We hurried toward the ship, passing tourists along the ramp. We had plenty of time to board, but it felt too good to be true—the Jamaica colors, the open ship, and the smiling crew that greeted us as we boarded.

Down narrow hallways, we found our cabin, and I opened the glass sliding doors to look out at the billowing water. It was a soft shade of blue, smooth as velvet. I stood there and took in the scent of the ocean, the Jamaica air. I watched the tourists hang out, their wide-brimmed hats and cocktails with wedges of pineapple or floating cherries. Eager, elated. I thought of all the stories we'd tell Wes's family and mine. How we'd reminisce about the fun we had at the wedding and joke about our honeymoon adventure. We'd pass out trinkets and postcards we bought at pricey little gift shops. We'd show them photos of the mountains, the shanties, the herds of goats roaming the streets. We'd play the videos we took on the ship: me with a tropical drink the size of a fishbowl, wearing a bright orange Jamaica sweatshirt and singing a Michael Jackson song; and Wes laughing, scanning the outdoor deck, the waterslides and pool party happening around us. But there would be no honeymoon talk with Mom. No T-shirt, keychain, or beaded jewelry. No shot glass, bottle of banana rum, or scenic postcard for the mother who missed her daughter's wedding.

Chapter 9

Plucking Petals

G randma was not a gardener, but things grew behind her little house with the yellow door. A smattering of white bricks sank into the earth like clean shoes. Between them, vines stretched and bent, crawled together like dancing legs. There were mint leaves, and Jesse taught me to pluck them and hold them on my tongue. To feel the tingle of flavor in my mouth. We played a game with flower petals, the daisy game. I plucked them slowly and tossed them to the ground, one by one: *She loves me. She loves me not.*

As an adult, I played this game with my memory. Sometimes when I couldn't sleep, I thought of Mom and motherhood, how it is an impossible role with standards too high to reach. How our worst memories bob to the surface while the good ones sink into our brains, making it easy for children to rehash their mother's failures. But this is the science of how memory works—a process we can't control. The purpose is to help us avoid recurring injury. We remember the fires that burn us. But my mother is more than a flame.

I've tried to understand her, to conjure buried memories.

I've closed my eyes and spoken to the space between my bones, the place where memories hide. My body is a history book.

I called Jesse. "Do you remember her being maternal... like taking us to the park, reading us books, or giving us hugs?" I waited for her, my encyclopedia sister. She thought for a moment, then recited the facts.

"The only thing I remember is, when I got upset, Mom would come into my room when I was crying. She'd tell me to hug her, and then she would say, 'Tighter, tighter, tighter.' That's the only thing I really remember her doing that was maternal. She was sensitive, but only when it came to *him*. She was worried about him, not us, and when he would come home, when he pulled in the driveway, she would tell us, 'Go, go, go. Go upstairs.' She would send us away."

When she said this, I saw my mom in my bedroom, hovering over me. I felt her arms moving stiffly around me, like a rope securing a load of cargo. I remembered thinking on these rare and awkward occasions when she solicited a hug that I didn't want love this way because it felt like obligation. And I knew even then that the hug was not for me. We were hugging her guilty conscience.

At forty-one, I was still learning how to accept a hug.

I closed my eyes again, went back to the garden, back in time to play the daisy game. . . .

She loves me. . . .

I was pregnant with my first son at twenty, curled on my bed, teary-eyed and limp as a headache hammered at the base of my skull. These were the headaches of my youth, the ones that left me flattened in the backseat of my mother's rust-colored station wagon, pinching my eyes shut as if to squeeze the pain out through my face. I recalled the salt and sting of hot tears in those elementary school years, the sound of rain pelting the car window as Mom's wiper blades squeaked and moaned, an agonizing sound. *Please*, I begged my mother, as if she could turn off the hammer in my head. She took me to doctors who ran tests and scans on my brain. She cut my long hair when a nurse said the hair might be the problem. But even with my thick braids gone, my hair a mass of curls like a well-watered Chia pet, the headaches persisted.

And then they stopped. For years, I stayed headache-free. But now with pregnancy hormones surging through my body, the hammer was back in full swing. My husband told me to take something—any over-the-counter remedy that would help. He searched the medicine cabinet and brought me a bottle of chalky white pills. "I can't," I told him. "The baby."

I whispered to my body and my child. We were one. I imagined my words echoing through the walls of my womb. The sound of my voice reaching my unborn baby nestled inside me, beneath the thud of my heartbeat. He was the size of an avocado, and yet . . . the size of everything.

The pain left me desperate for my mother, and I called to my husband, "Go get her."

I couldn't understand why I needed her so urgently, but I did. When she arrived, I heard her footsteps climbing the stairs. She reached my bed and sat on the edge of the mattress and stroked my head. Coming from her, the gesture felt like a tremendous gift.

"Why does it hurt like this?" I asked, as if I were my child self again, begging my mother for answers.

"There's a lot happening right now—in your body," she said in a soft, diplomatic tone. "Think of all the work that's being done to make all those little bones and features."

She loves me not. . . .

I sat at the table with my math homework, numbers swirling in my ten-year-old mind, making me dizzy. Mom stood behind me, watching me grip my pencil. It hovered over the page, and I couldn't make it move. My grandma said math made her brain freeze, and I thought we were alike in this way. But my mother had a mind like a calculator and she was impatient, shifting from foot to foot. The numbers glared at me, and I couldn't make sense of the math. Mom slammed her hand down on the table and leaned in to yell in my ear.

"You are stupid, so stupid." Her voice shot into the air like an arrow from a bow. It traveled through me and then through time, where it would swim in my ears for three decades, pound in my head like rain on a lake. Her words became the lake, and that is how a voice becomes a truth—even when it's a lie.

She loves me. . . .

I was in kindergarten, or maybe first grade. My mother sang a song, standing in the light of the bathroom, gazing in the mirror. She picked up a tube of mascara, pink as bubblegum, and unscrewed the green cap. I watched her pump the wand, once, twice, three times, before pulling it away from the tube. She angled her face in the light and cracked her mouth open in a concentrated O. She wriggled the tiny black brush through her lashes, then stood back to examine her work. She was an artist, I thought, or a beauty queen. Mom smelled like vanilla musk and her hair was dyed red. Sometimes it was blond, or black, or somewhere in between. Shoulder length and thick, coiled at the edges, the shape of her barrel rollers. I wanted to squeeze her fat curls and pet them like a puppy or a kitten. She turned to me and motioned me into the bathroom. Her face was bright and firm, shimmering with color. She began grooming me, and it was not like the hurried mornings before school when she yanked my unruly hair into pigtails so tight my eyes went slant. On those days, I waited until she was out of sight and I worked my fingers around the elastic hair ties, wiggling them loose until my face felt like my face again and not a rubber band. Now, she was gentle.

"Close your eyes," she said, and I felt the soft stroke of a makeup brush on my skin. I was the luckiest girl, standing beneath the bathroom lights with my mother's attention on me, her perfume wafting like a hug, her hands intent on my face. I smiled a huge smile. "Stay still." I was her canvas that day. When she had painted me to perfection, she hoisted me up in front of the mirror. My face was a rainbow of color and I looked like a woman or a doll, a dark-haired Barbie.

Mom sent me off to play, and I skipped outside to feel the sun on my pretty new face. All I could do was smile because I couldn't believe how pretty I was. Pretty like my mother.

She loves me not. . . .

My husband began disappearing on nights when he wasn't at work. Twenty-two and alone in our apartment with a toddler and a newborn, I called my mother. She had moved south a few years prior and had not seen us since. I could only describe my new baby boy, his round head a flutter of dark hair and the smell of his warm neck as he napped.

"I'm lonely," she said, and it mirrored the way I felt. I'd had just one visitor at the hospital, Aunt Rachel. But my husband was estranged from his family, and I had no mother to bring me hot meals, to relieve me for a nap, or to help me adjust to life with two sons, as is the custom for postpartum moms.

Day after day, I called Mom in a panic over my missing husband. I knew he was breaking away, that our marriage was tumbling toward the end, and I would soon be completely alone, a single mom. It was just a matter of time.

"Move here," Mom urged. "Just pack up and move here." And it seemed like the quickest possible fix. A change of scenery, a change of pace. When I posed the question one day, I'm not sure why my husband agreed. He was tired of our monotony, but willing to make a change and see where it led. We sold our furniture and loaded up our car with kids and clothes and everything we could cram in around us. We drove south to start something new. To *be* something new.

When I think of this now, my chest caves in on my breath. I was moving into a house with my childhood monster, my children and husband in tow. But the years of pretending had altered my sense of reality.

I could learn to live with him again, I reasoned—just until we got established. My husband had heard stories about my stepdad, but they seemed like mere myths to him now. I told myself the move was a good idea. Because of my loneliness, because of the feeling that gravity had gone away, and maybe my mother could help me find it. Maybe Mom could save me as never before. I needed to give her the chance.

When we arrived, Mom was ecstatic. She showed us the two bedrooms and bathroom we would use at the opposite end of the house. The tidy room the boys would share with green curtains and a large window with a view of the backyard. Our room was larger, with a television, a cherrywood cabinet and a black lacquer dresser with an Asian flair. Mom had painted the living room red, reupholstered a bench, hung sheer curtains, placed silk pillows on the sofas and decorated the walls with Asian and African art. Painted wooden masks, ornate tapestries, and vibrant, elaborate vases. She swept us through each room like a tour guide. "Isn't this beautiful?" she said of a standing lamp, fingering its crystal pendants.

The boys clung to my husband and me, and we took them outside, and I rocked my babies on the swing in the sunshine. My husband sipped cans of cold soda and smiled. He scouted the area for new pizza joints, parks, and places to shop. The new atmosphere kept him occupied. In the early mornings when my stepdad had gone to work, Mom crept to our end of the house and retrieved my squirming infant. She bathed him, diapered him, dressed him, and tickled him while I poured my first cup of coffee and peeled a banana for KJ. I was elated with Mom's efforts. I so desperately wanted her to be a grandmother like the one I had in my childhood, an ally for my children.

Within weeks, I was working at a ramshackle health center across town while my husband stayed home with the boys. The center was a gloomy place with feeble bodies curled up like kicked dogs. There was a woman's ward with six patients in one room, and I had to shimmy around the row of beds and raise them by hand with a crank. Everything squeaked and moaned: the patients, the equipment, and the staff. The place was always muggy, and the rancid smells seeped into my pores. I took long showers when I returned home, but I never felt clean enough.

The tension kept building between Mom and her husband. I realized he didn't want us around. In fact, he hadn't known we were coming at all. Mom pretended it was all a surprise. She didn't tell him it was her idea, because she was lonely, because she wanted her daughter nearby. When we entered the kitchen, he turned and left, muttered and slammed things around. One day, he didn't return from work, and my mother discovered his closet was empty. She flew across the house, opening drawers and cupboards and doors, searching for additional clues. My husband and I watched, babies bouncing on our hips.

"He left me. He fucking left me," she screeched, then disappeared into her bedroom on the other side of the house. My husband and I arched our eyebrows and moved toward the kitchen. We filled pots with water to boil noodles and stirred dinner over the stove. When the food was hot, I stood with a plate at my mother's door, ready to gingerly knock. Instead I listened. She was on the telephone, sobbing and pleading. She told her husband she was sorry we came; it was a big mistake. "Just come home. Come home."

After dinner when we lay in bed, I told my husband what I'd heard. His face sharpened. I could see he was thinking about what to do next. He stared at the ceiling for a while, silent.

A few weeks passed, and we developed a new evening routine: me cooking dinner, my husband scowling, and my mother sinking deeper into despair. She disappeared into her bedroom and made frenzied calls at night. "Come home. Come home," she pleaded.

She moved stiffly through the house. She stopped talking, eating, and grandmothering my little boys. I felt we were holding her hostage, my criminal sons and me. I watched her face, sagging with sorrow. I told her to eat, please eat, but her dinner sat cold every night. Starvation was her official protest. She'd lost an alarming amount of weight in those short weeks. Her silhouette was a gaunt resemblance to the woman who greeted us when we first arrived.

I had nothing to return to, no apartment, no job, no plan. I wanted to stay and make a life with my mother, but I knew it was time to head north. It was my husband who took the first step. One evening in the middle of dinner, he watched her slump at the table. He frowned, then flew out of his chair, and rushed to the bedroom to pack.

When we'd gathered everything and reloaded it into our car, my husband was sweaty and my sons were wailing. I noticed my mother's shining demeanor, the glow of relief in her eyes. She hurried toward the kitchen cabinet, and it was the fastest she'd moved in weeks. She reached up to retrieve a forgotten item: a baby bottle. There were no hugs, kisses, or lengthy goodbyes. I climbed into the waiting car, leaned into my seat, and watched my mother in the doorway, standing straighter already.

She loves me. . . .

We arrived in Milwaukee with nowhere to stay, so we checked into a motel with rates by the week. It was a bleak place, with stiff orange bedspreads, formica counters, and a toilet that never stopped running. But the rooms were cheap, and we paid with the little cash we had while I hunted for more permanent places.

During a tour of a two-bedroom upper with a stern-faced landlord, KJ got excited and stomped up the steps. The man stopped walking and snapped, "This is a quiet building and I plan to keep it that way." My husband squeezed KJ's hand while I attempted to shush the babbling baby. When we returned to the car, he berated me for dragging us out in the cold. But I continued my search, and a month later we landed a decent place with sunny rooms and a tidy green backyard. By this time, I was beyond desperate, and the tender landlord softened when I teared up and apologized on behalf of my rowdy sons. I wondered if he had a daughter my age, a sister, or maybe a secretary. He smiled, gestured toward the yard and said, "There's plenty of space for little ones to play back here."

Working opposite shifts as we'd always done, my husband and I spent little time together and regarded each other as roommates. Two haggard parents, passing in the hall on the way to the shower, the bedroom, or the kitchen. Working double shifts at a new health center followed by the tasks of mothering our boys left me empty, exhausted, and with zero affection to spare. At first, my husband resented the fact that a cozy novel and a hot cup of coffee appealed to me more than time alone with him. Later, it became a permission slip to sneak off with another woman.

We argued. Resentments grew like a fungus on our marriage. One winter night, I was overly tired and irritable. This time when my husband berated me, he called me a bitch, and I finally snapped. I rose up like a poked bear, striking one physical blow after another at my husband. My hands and feet moved like wild propellers, slapping, kicking, and unleashing my rage. Instinctively, he covered his face and body, protecting himself from me. It thrilled me for a moment, then shocked me back to fear. I stood next to him in our living room, feeling my courage drain as his hands dropped back to his sides and the force of my actions registered on his face. Clad in flannel pajamas and a pair of tattered slippers, I grabbed my car keys and cell phone and fled.

It was dark as I slid down the frozen streets in our burgundy Malibu. I had the feeling that I was lost in my own neighborhood. Where does a woman go in flannel pajamas after she's pummeled her husband? I saw the hot clouds of my breath in the car, but I didn't click on the heater. I wanted to be numb. When I pulled into a grocery store parking lot, I was crying. The tears overwhelmed my body, a hurricane of shame shaking and rattling my bones. It didn't occur to me that the people who should love me most had betrayed me—my husband with his mistress, my mother with my stepdad. Suddenly, it was all too much. They had chosen other people, other lives. They held me at a distance. And for this, I could only feel shame.

On my cell phone, I dialed Mom's number and felt a sense of relief as the ringing filled my ear. It was late, and I imagined her groggy on the sofa in front of a movie she'd fallen asleep to. Her husband had returned, and their lives were back to normal. Back to the bliss of a life without her daughter and grandkids. When she finally picked up, her voice was strained. "What's wrong?"

She sounded concerned, like a very good mother. The kind of woman who listens and loves. I stumbled through my story, my chest heaving, and head aching. I felt small and helpless, but Mom's voice was comforting, grounding. I imagined myself, an anguished patient reaching out to grab a nurse's hair. *Let me out. Let me out.*

I don't recall what she said, only that it was what I needed to hear. She didn't gripe about the burden of my call, the late hour or the foolishness of my actions toward my husband. She didn't say, *You're making a bad situation worse.* Or, *He could have killed you, you know? He's much stronger and you've seen his violent temper. What were you thinking?*

She was calm, empathetic. She was exactly the mother I needed.

She loves me not. . . .

I was sitting in my cold car, watching the heater melt the ice on my windshield. I called Mom to tell her I just worked a sixteen-hour shift at the health center. It was early morning, and I needed her to keep me awake. "Just talk to me while I drive home," I said.

It was four years since we left Mom's home in a fury. She

and my stepdad had moved to a new house in Florida, and she'd begun prodding me to move there too. The past was repeating itself, but somehow I failed to see it. Mom was pouring her second cup of coffee. An early riser, she said she'd done a load of wash and cleaned the blades on her ceiling fans. "You can't believe how filthy they get. It's disgusting."

I maneuvered my car out of the parking lot. The snow was fresh, and my headlights made it sparkle like mounds of white opal. Soon I'd be in my pajamas, slipping beneath the blankets for a half day of sleep. It was the year before my divorce, and I still had a husband at home. On the weekends after my night shifts, I slept while he kept our young boys busy with movies, wrestling matches and little cars on plastic tracks. When I woke up in the early afternoons, I'd drag myself into the kitchen and begin collecting the crusty cereal bowls and juice cups, sluggish and drowsy.

My husband's other life was a mystery, and there was always trouble when I asked where he went, what he did. I learned to keep my mouth shut. When he appeared in the doorway, he was breathtakingly handsome in his jeans, football jersey, and clean sneakers. I thought of the way he used to cherish me, the way he looked at me admiringly. His thick hair so black it shone, like his eyes. Now he was ready to leave the moment I stepped out of bed. "Mom's up, boys," he told our rowdy sons. "Go ask her for lunch."

In my car, navigating the snow-slick roads, I pushed away thoughts of my husband and our problems at home. I snapped back to my mother's voice. "It's really good," she says. "Not like regular yogurt at all—really fluffy." She was raving about the new whipped yogurt she discovered at the grocery store. "Strawberry is good, but so is vanilla."

"I'll give it a shot," I said. We paused for a moment. I watched the stoplight change from red to green, and I slowly laid on the gas. My car sloshed forward on the mushy road.

"Don't forget to send Dad a card," Mom said. I felt my hands tighten on the wheel. Her spiel burned in my stomach. It was the same every year, on birthdays, holidays, Father's Day and others. She insisted I buy the man cards and trinkets, and when I did, it was because I wanted to make *her* happy. It was my job to make everyone happy. My husband, my children, my mother. It was a small gesture, a piece of paper, a card, and if I could drop it in the mail, I could keep the peace. It occurred to me that every time I gave in, I buried my truth a little deeper.

That year, with my marriage crashing toward the end, I was finding bits of courage. Instead of a card for her husband, I wrote a letter to Mom. Every line was a momentous struggle and tears fell on the pages as I scrolled the words in black ink. Again and again, I wrote my letters, then tore each one up and started again. It hurt to write, but it felt good too. Easier than standing in the card aisle at the store and picking through the selection of greetings to *Dearest Daddy*, *a Very Special Man*, or *My Beloved Father*. Every card felt ridiculous in my hands and I tried to think of the good things he did. I tried to be positive. My stepdad had repaired my broken bikes, driven me to school some days, and brought home paychecks to help support the family. But when I thought of his violence, fear leaped out from the shadows of my memory. I saw my stepdad at the head of the table, lunging from his chair, slapping me to the floor. I saw his naked form in my bedroom. My attempts to suppress these thoughts only brought them back with a vengeance. There was a broken girl inside me, and her edges were sharpening my pain.

I penned my letter to Mom: *I need you to understand that I can't keep pretending, not even to spare your feelings. The cards and gifts are a lie. He did terrible things to me, to our family. How can I call him Dad? I know what it means to forgive, but I'll never forget. You made a choice to stay married and keep him in our lives. As a child, I had to live with that decision because we don't get to choose our parents. But I'm an adult now, and I have the power to say I've had enough.*

When the letter reached Mom, it all blew up in my face. What kind of daughter was I? How could I write those things? I felt instant remorse as she wailed into the phone and then threatened suicide. I betrayed her. Why couldn't I be kinder, more compassionate and forgiving?

My husband was slipping away, and I couldn't bear to lose Mom too. I returned to the store. I bought a card, something bland and impersonal. It was just $3.00—the price of my mother's love.

She loves me. . . .

After my divorce and some years of back and forth with my ex-husband, I decided Florida was a place for fresh starts. The boys said their goodbyes, hugging and high-fiving their dad, and we moved into a cozy little house in my mother's neighborhood. I'd buried the memories of our former troubles. The years had passed, and I'd discovered a church that preached forgiveness, a doctrine that eased my heart. I took my sons to church and prayed I was the mother they deserved, a woman they could be proud of.

KJ made friends immediately, but Sym was a raging bull. His teen years became increasingly hard, and I bore the brunt of his anger simply because of proximity. We always hurt the ones closest to us.

He pounded his fists into his bedroom walls, and I didn't know how to stop the blows. I tried talking, but he said, "Get the hell out of my room."

I tried yelling, but it only led to hoarse voices. I cried, prayed, and cried and prayed again. I took our little dog on short walks at night and wondered if the distance between God and me was just too great, and if prayers got lost in the stars. I watched the sky, counting the specks of gold, the distant matter. Was a mother with a broken son distant matter too?

The next day, I walked to my mother's house for coffee and a chat, a break. Within minutes, I heard Sym slam her front door. He burst in and glared at me. He was fourteen, tall and lanky, and when I looked into his brown eyes I wondered how he could be both my beautiful son and a perfect stranger. A boy and a wild beast.

He picked up where we left off arguing. He *needed* his video games. He was a gamer; didn't I understand? Our voices clashed like swords in Mom's living room. My hands shook around my coffee mug as he edged closer, yelled louder.

"You will not talk to my daughter like that in my house," my mother blasted. Startled, Sym and I fell silent. I was in awe of Mom. She stood in the doorway, a pillar, a warrior with curlers in her hair and sagging pajamas. I heard an unfamiliar strain in her voice as she continued to rip at my son. "Your mother works hard. Your mother takes good care of you. How dare you?"

Her words were quick, but they came from a deep well of emotion. They were thick with feeling, sharp with intent. I thought I would never forget the words, or her fury in that moment. Her fury on my behalf.

One year later, with a surge of teen hormones and a rage too big for his body, Sym attempted suicide for the first time, and it was my mother who sat by my side at the hospital. Her hands firm in her lap, she was silent. There were many things I wished to hear from her, but at that moment, I treasured her silence. We were silent together, two flawed mothers. And everything else was distant matter.

Chapter 10

Making Space

Secrets can make you sick. My sister never told the authorities what our stepdad did to her—unthinkable things. Throughout the years, her recollections remained vivid, while I repressed mine. My mind, a television set stuck between channels, played only fuzzy bits of the past. I saw the man's hands in the swimming pool, I smelled his sweaty hair in summer, felt the fear that throbbed within me like a separate heartbeat. It thumped loudest at night and in the afternoons when it was just us in the house. In winter, I stared at my snow-stained boots near the door, thinking I could put them on and run to Grandma's house. I could tell her everything. But it didn't happen that way.

In my memory, I saw my mother in the blur of her busyness, flying through the house collecting laundry or counting change for school lunches. I heard the sound of her hairspray in the morning, the can clunking down on the bathroom counter. The jingle of her keys. The relief of her presence after work, the smell of her leather bag. "I'm tired now, go to your room."

These dim and colorless memories circled the edges of my mind. They were vague, as if they belonged to another girl in another place and time, which, of course, they had. In contrast,

my sister's trauma was a spotlight that never dimmed, an agonizing beam on her conscience. Her guilt plagued her with
questions: wasn't she the big sister, and shouldn't she have protected her siblings? Shouldn't she have protected herself? She
was a *child*, victimized and traumatized—a fact she often forgot.

When I thought of Jesse, I recalled her courage. She'd pelted
our stepdad with dolls and stuffed bears when he crept into our
shared bedroom at night, a child's ammunition. She screamed
for Mom, who only occasionally woke up, but never got out of
bed. From her bedroom down the hall, Mom would call for her
husband with a groggy voice, "Come back to bed. Come back
to bed." What did she think he'd been doing? What excuses
did he make?

In our teen years, Jesse pulled a knife on my stepfather and
held it between us in the kitchen. Once, as punishment for
running away from home, he'd threatened to cut my long hair.
But that day, she threatened to cut his throat.

She was a fighter, and we had our battles too—sisterly spats.
We tussled in the basement over clothing she stole from my
closet: my black checkered skirt or maxi dresses. I slapped and
clawed at her face, and she slammed me against the grandfather
clock in the basement den. I was quick to forgive, but she was
not. Later, if I showed up at the Golly's where she worked, she'd
open the drive-thru window and splash me with a Green River
soda. I'd stand there dripping, sticky with summer heat and
fountain soda, staring in disbelief at the pool of green liquid on
the sidewalk. She was allowed to treat me this way, but no one
else could. Not a high school bully or my own snotty friends. If
anyone crossed me, Jesse was ready for a brawl.

When a friend called to say our brother, Joey, was in a fight
at the fair, Jesse and I rushed to the kitchen to grab a pair of
knives. We ran more than a mile to St. Gregory's church festival

that night, the sound of our sneakers stomping on the dark sidewalks as we gripped our weapons, huffed, and panted. But when we got there, the grounds were packed with teens in line to ride the Tilt-A-Whirl or toss balls at a stack of tin jugs. We searched the crowds with our kitchen blades tucked into our jeans, ready to defend our little brother. But Joey wasn't there.

That wasn't the first time we'd sprung into action this way, and neither would it be the last. That winter, a skinhead threatened Joey. He'd been driving by and saw the three of us walking—Joey, Jesse, and me. He slowed his black Thunderbird, lowered his window, and shouted in my brother's direction, "Fucking spics."

Joey threw his hands up in the air, and the car screeched to a stop in the middle of the empty road. The skinhead stepped out, a pale lanky man with droopy eyes. His male passenger had a shaved head too, although his head was round with a lump of fat near the nape of his neck. The first man wore a heavy metal T-shirt and a trench coat. He held his pockets out at his sides, which made his black coat look like a pair of bat wings. He'd left his motor idling, and the car sputtered behind him while he stood beside a glazed mound of snow. Joey laughed when he threatened us, and he called the man's bluff. It happened so fast, and then fists were flying. I was scared for my brother, although I had no reason to believe he would lose the fight. Joey was a force in his adolescent years. Without thinking, I leaped up and pulled the guy down by the back of his neck. Jesse began kicking him in the face, chin, and torso. His fat-necked friend never left the passenger seat, only watched as three "spics" pounded the skinhead on that icy street in Milwaukee.

Joey had moved out of state, and Jesse was in her twenties with two kids when she found our estranged dad. Her life was a whirlwind like mine, and occasionally we got together to let our kids chase one another in the yard while we divvied up snacks and doled out threats.

"Put that stick down, KJ. . ." I'd start to say.

"Before your momma beats some sense into you," Jesse would interject.

Always the leader between us, she'd used her sarcasm to discipline my sons. And they found it outrageously funny, but terrifying too. When my nephew misbehaved and she told him to "go play in traffic," he chuckled. But I could see my sons register shock, their little faces searching the road as cars zoomed by at high speed. I was a gentler disciplinarian, and my sons were church-going sheltered little boys. Eventually, they understood Jesse's jokes and learned to banter with her.

With Dad in her life, Jesse was brash and witty as always, and the two got along like old friends. It was strange at first, how they fit like pieces of a puzzle. When I think of their bond, I see Dad's face, his head tossed back, yielding to laughter as Jesse hurled her jokes. The moment is stuck in my memory like a bookmark wedged between pages. Pages of a history we'll never relive.

Dad and I didn't have a relationship. I'd waited for him all my life, watched fathers with their children and wondered what it would be like. When he finally emerged as if from a dream, I was distracted by my falling-apart marriage. But we'd chatted, and after seeing him with Jesse, I thought maybe I could have what they had. Wasn't I a piece of the same puzzle? We made plans and he'd promised to visit but never showed, leaving me watching the road, feeling the chill of wind on the front porch where I waited, waited, and waited with my little boys tugging at my sleeves.

Is he coming soon? What's taking so long?" That was enough for me. I was angry about all the nights I'd spent waiting for a husband who stayed out late, and where was my long-lost dad, another vanishing man? I didn't have the capacity to feel more pain, and so I never gave him another chance. I didn't realize there'd be a day when chances disappeared.

Jesse didn't know the extent of Dad's cancer. She took him to the hospital on a Friday and a few days later, she texted me a photo of a man strung with tubes, a sagging figure in a hospital bed. The remnants of my father. It seemed so abrupt, the ding of my phone and the photo filling my screen. I was in my living room, watching evening television with Wes. Our dog Mia at our feet, pressed against the sofa, the sound of her snoring drowned out by an episode of *Bloodline*.

It was roughly four months after Wes and I were married, and we were settling into our days. Early mornings, work routines and evenings spent lounging in our pajamas, chattering over dinner and sharing a wedge of brie. We were as we always were: silly, happy, comfortable. Only now we shared a last name. When people asked, "How's married life?" I told them it was good. "Life is good." I said it with confidence, not knowing I was living the days and moments before my undoing. The collapse of a house made of cards. But Wes would be there to help me pick it all up.

When the text came, I thought about Jesse in a cold hospital in Wisconsin, me on my sofa watching TV, the Florida sun pulsing through the windows, and my father, slipping into death with my sister at his bedside. The contrast seemed cruel and unfair. My life had moved forward, while Jesse's seemed stuck on repeat. A cycle of trauma, loss, pain. She'd been married and divorced several times, endured financial ruin, and mental health problems upon problems. When would it get better for her?

She told me she cried at Dad's bedside, begged him to give her more time. But it was too late. It was no longer him in that hospital bed. Dad was tethered to life via tubes, a puppet held up by its strings. Jesse found the strength to release him, and it must have been the hardest decision she'd ever made. The decision to end your Dad's life. He was just sixty-one.

I imagined Jesse with physical and tangible baggage. I thought of her waking up with sadness and sorrow, with dark-rimmed eyes still blurry with pain. I wondered if the sights and even the smells of death and loss stayed with her. I thought of her trying to do normal tasks, like frying Mexican rice in her kitchen, the hot oil and garlic mingling with the memory of the antiseptic hospital odors, and the place where she said goodbye to Dad. She'd shown me a photo of him working the grill at some outdoor park or backyard gathering in Milwaukee. She said he was a master griller. I imagined her now, watching a cloud of smoke envelop the man behind the grill. Would she always see Dad's face in the haze, and would the aroma of charcoal and flames forever trigger the memory of him forking and flipping cooked meats? The image of him smiling at her?

When I heard the phrase "grief is a multitasking emotion," I considered how this works. How I'd felt gutted, lost, and utterly abandoned after my first husband and I divorced. I walked around in a state of confusion. I learned how to wake up alone, how to face the day as a single woman, a single mother, a person who'd been blasted with the gunfire of betrayal. I wondered what had happened to my life, and if the bleeding would ever stop. But life doesn't stop, so I hobbled forward and found short bursts of relief, moments of forgetting followed by hours of forgetting, days of forgetting, and finally, the distance to wave at the dark hole that grief had become in my rearview mirror. But losing a marriage is not like losing a parent, a dad. I know that life will interrupt Jesse's grief, giving her occasional relief so she can sleep, shower, work, and eat. But her pain will be permanent. It will shrink and expand, shrink and expand, in her heart like a song from the bellows of an accordion.

I planned to attend the funeral, then decided that packing a bag, booking a flight, and picking an outfit was too much. My body didn't want to move. So I took three days off from work and sat in the empty house with my empty self. I wore a ratty T-shirt with a pair of bleach-stained pants. I watched my chest rise and fall. Suddenly, I needed this proof that I existed. My sister texted me more photos of our dad, and I stared at his eyes until their black depth sucked me back in time.

One picture showed Dad posing with his face pressed to my sister's. Two cheeks that would never touch again in real life. I couldn't stop thinking about what might have been. The questions I might have asked him, all of the things that weren't possible anymore. The door of possibilities had slammed shut forever.

"My dad is dead. My dad is dead," I said out loud, thinking the repetition might make it less of a shock.

When Marie called to check on me, the phone sounded strange when it rang.

"Hello?" I'd said, as if it were the middle of the night and not the middle of the day. Marie asked how I was feeling. She said she was thinking of me.

"Don't forget to lean on Wes. I'm glad you two have each other."

I remembered this that night when I lay in bed next to my husband. He kissed my lips and then drifted away, leaving only the wind of his breath between us. I knew I should have curled up beside him for warmth. I should have done as Marie suggested—lean on my husband. But sometimes pain is a solitary thing, too complex and personal to share. I didn't know what to feel, think, say. Life stopped feeling real all at once.

When I returned to work, I sat at my desk and heard the office banter. My coworkers talked about their spouses and children and where they might eat lunch that day. *Who wants Japanese?* Their voices warbled, as though underwater, but I knew I was the one who was sinking below the surface. Pushed down by the weight of emotions, I worked myself to exhaustion in the effort to stay afloat. I stared at the blank document on my computer screen. Writing used to be a life raft, but that day it couldn't save me from the grief.

Around noon, I walked outside and my body cut a path through the heat, repelling everything as if by magnetic force. I thought about how fed-up people sometimes want to run away, but I didn't have it in me to run. Instead, I wanted to fall away, like a woman stepping off a ledge.

When I found my car, I got inside and drove to a spot that was shaded by a low-hanging tree. I cracked my windows and reminded my body to breathe. *Breathe. Breathe.* When my cell phone rang, the number lit up on the screen. It was a therapist, and this was our first session. It had been many years since I talked to a therapist. She asked if it was a good time to chat.

"Yes," I answered without hesitation.

"Well, I want to thank you for reaching out and let you know I'm listening." She paused, cleared her throat and began again. Her voice was suffused with compassion, compassion for a stranger. "Tell me what compelled you to make this appointment," she said.

I saw people toting lunch bags or rushing off in groups. Life was swimming all around me, but I was a lonesome fish locked in a murky tank. "My dad died," I answered.

"I'm sorry," she replied, and from her tone I could tell she meant it. I knew what was required of me next. I needed to tell her how this made me feel. How could I explain something I didn't understand?

"I barely knew him," I said. She was silent as I caught my breath, and I thought of the way Wes and I paused for Marie. For her grief, as she told a story about the man she loved for most of her life, her husband. I felt foolish. I didn't have the right to this response. My father was not significant to my life.

I kept talking, hoping an explanation or maybe a solution might somehow tumble out.

"A death can open old wounds," she said. "Could it be that you're reliving some childhood trauma?"

This frightened me. I wanted to be a woman who took life as it came. I didn't want to live in the past. I told the therapist about Wes, our wedding, the bliss, my sons, my job, and my mom. The conversation turned then, and I felt anger crawl up my spine. Mom. . . .

After an hour of ranting, I hung up the phone and walked back to work. I would go through the motions until I could feel normal again.

I found sympathy cards in the mail from Wes's family. His mother, sister, and daughter all sent their prayers and encouragement. These sentiments showed me who cared. But more importantly, they reminded me who didn't. My bitterness toward Mom grew. At the same time, I hated myself for wanting her affection, for expecting the impossible. Nurturing was a hopeless thing to want from my mother. Why should she care that my father died? I wanted her to consider the loss I was experiencing, to acknowledge my right to grieve. Dad's death had forced me to think about the parental connection, the depth of the imprint he both left and didn't leave. But also, I thought about Mom because she was the only parent I had left. I was mourning both death and life. Dad and Mom.

I visited Aunt Rachel on my way home from work. She stood in front of her kitchen pantry, examining stacked packages of tea and instant cappuccino. "English Toffee or Mocha?" she asked.

"Toffee," I said, dropping my purse on the floor near the couch. Her little gray terrier sniffed my legs, then plopped down on the rug in the center of the room. I watched him lick and nip the scruff around his paws.

"Your sister's not doing well," Aunt Rachel said, reaching for two mugs in the cabinet. "I sent her flowers. I keep telling your mother she's hurting. She needs to call her." Aunt Rachel shook her head. "You would think. . . ." She started again, then stopped to discipline the dog, who had hopped up beside me and spread himself out on the couch.

I reminded Aunt Rachel of the text Mom sent me the night before my wedding: *Best wishes tomorrow.*

"Why do we expect so much from her?" I said, burying my hand in the gray fur now splayed across my lap. "She's one-dimensional. A drugstore card." I chuckled at my joke, but sadness flickered in my chest. My sister deserved maternal compassion. She deserved a mother. *We* deserved a mother.

At home, I found a photo of my dad leaning against the hood of an 80s minivan. I didn't know where it came from or how it got shoved inside the box with the ones of my sons, images of them in winter coats, hoods pulled tight around their wind-burned faces, Midwestern snow high and white. I thought I remembered Dad the way I remembered my sons, with the same clarity and familiarity, but I couldn't be sure if I did, or if it were even possible. Perhaps all I really had were the second-hand stories I'd heard from Jesse and Aunt Rachel. It frustrated me to think that Mom had so much knowledge about him, so many memories. But she'd let her personal hatred muddy their entire history. I grew up knowing I could never so much as allude to the fact that her husband was not my own flesh and blood, not my *real* father.

I stared at my photo of Dad, trying to get a sense of him, to hold onto a slippery memory. When I checked the mail that evening, a letter had arrived on his behalf. The letterhead said *Pension Fund* in dark green ink. I scanned the page and stopped at Dad's name, followed by the word "deceased." It trailed his name like some kind of designation, impersonal, clinical. A lab-coat-at-the-morgue kind of word, one you might see in a medical chart while reading about someone's withered brain-stem or pair of deflated lungs. But there it was. My dad was deceased.

I swallowed the word as time slowed to a thickening pace, a spoon stirring honey. I glanced out the kitchen window in an effort to ground myself. Every neighbor with a dog had claimed the grassy lot beside our house and deemed it pooping ground. Whenever I stood near the window to load the dishwasher or water the succulents I kept on the ledge, I'd see a Labrador squatting or a fluffy white mixed breed sniffing the grass at his owner's feet, the owner's bald head pink as a grapefruit. Some-times I saw the overweight English bulldog that lived on the other side of the lot. I'd always wanted to scoop up his chin and pull his face to mine so I could kiss the wide space between his eyes and see his sour mug up close. Bulldogs were irresistible that way, their permanent pout and lazy waddle. This dog was indeed a waddler, with a belly that grazed the ground.

I watched a Chihuahua explore the lot, a newcomer. I won-dered if the spunky little guy was a cuddler like the Chihuahua I'd owned years ago. I wondered if he yapped at strangers with the same needle-sharp pitch or bit the wind on cold days, as if he could punish Mother Nature for his misery. Whenever I heard the term "cold snap," I imagined my Chihuahua's little mouth snapping at the winter wind.

When the owner tugged the dog away from the lot, I returned to my letter, wondering what else I needed to know about my "deceased" father. As I read, I learned I was entitled to receive a survivor's benefit from his pension fund, and that the total sum would be split among my siblings and me. The amount was insignificant, but the money didn't matter as much as the letter in my hand, a parting gift from my actual father. Suddenly it felt like something concrete, something more intimate than a mysterious photo.

I thought about Dad's work history, his slew of jobs over the years. He'd worked at a meat packing plant, at a company that manufactured tools and transportation equipment, and the last I'd heard, he'd segued to construction jobs. He'd just come back from Guam during the brief time when we'd reconnected so long ago. He'd been putting roofs on buildings, and he said it was backbreaking work, hot and hard. But Guam was amazing, he raved. He showed me a photo he'd kept folded in his blue jeans pocket like some kind of good luck token. In the picture, he held a long, slick fish in both hands. His skin was a shade darker from long days in the heat, almost brown-burgundy against his white teeth. He stood on a sandy shore with the backdrop of breathtakingly vivid water, a turquoise gemstone rolled out like a rug.

That year I attended a company Christmas party hosted by his employer. I picked Dad up in my new Dodge Neon and drove in the haze of a snowstorm to an elaborate lodge in Kenosha, Wisconsin, where a giant moose head hung above the lobby fireplace. I wondered why taxidermy had ever become decor. I nodded sympathetically to the moose for the unfortunate state of his skull. Dad was all smiles that day, shaking hands with the corporate bigwigs and introducing me, proud of his daughter. I wore a baby blue dress that was long and shimmery, flecked with silver that danced in the light. We stood in the banquet hall where hundreds of staff members mingled. It smelled like baked chicken, gravy, and expensive perfume. I looked around nervously at all the white tablecloths and polished serving dishes. These affairs always made me self-conscious, and I shifted in my pinched shoes pretending to know where to put my hands. Had anyone else invited me, I would have politely declined, using some excuse about not having a sitter or wanting to keep my schedule open for a potential overtime shift at the hospital. But it was my dad who had invited me, and it seemed like my duty to go, to make an effort to build a rapport. That was before the real drama had begun with my then-husband, and before I gave up on Dad and let him drift back out of my life. Funny how I'd spent so many years longing for him, only to reject him when he missed an afternoon date.

But we shared a memory inside the crowded lodge, where the large windows were fogged with artificial heat. Dad wore a crisp collared shirt, and he was lean and confident like he'd been in the photo. His movements were easy and fluid, and watching him made me feel like a cardboard box, stiff and unimpressive. That was the Dad I wanted to remember, the banquet hall Dad showing off his daughter. There'd been very few occasions on which I felt like someone's daughter, on which I could openly, brazenly claim my real, blood-and-bones Dad. Now he was deceased, but I was still here, and this letter was proof of what he had been, despite the circumstances. For so long, I'd been trained, groomed, forced to lose this part of my identity, this familial link. But now I had a letter that said

I was "entitled" to something on behalf of my father. I *was* his daughter. It seemed to corroborate the truth I had never been permitted. Now I was holding it, and it was strangely affirming.

A week passed and then a second letter came, the one that would rearrange everything. It came with the same green letterhead as the first, the same introduction and greeting. This time, however, the words left me spinning. As I read it, I didn't pull myself away so I could ground myself in the moment or ponder the world outside my window. I didn't flash back to memories of the dinner I'd shared with Dad or his photos of Guam. Instead, I thought about Mom and all that she'd taken from me as my eyes bore into the words:

This letter serves as a follow-up to the previous letter regarding your eligibility to receive a survivor benefit from a pension fund. We regret to inform you that because we are now aware that you were adopted by a person other than the deceased, we are bound by Wisconsin law to exclude you from being a beneficiary. Please disregard the previous letter and any accompanying documents.

In all its brevity, what I gleaned from that letter was this: You are nobody's daughter. The rejection felt so familiar, as if my mother had typed the letter. And then I thought of a scenario about home invasions, which related, but also didn't.

I'd never considered a housebreaking a life-changing tragedy. But then a friend shared her own experience. She'd come home on an ordinary day to find her home pilfered, destroyed—cracked picture frames, broken vases and family heirlooms. The pieces of a life so savagely discarded or stolen. The commercial for a home security system played in my mind, the somber music as the camera panned the busted furnishings and blank spaces where a television or stereo once stood. The gaping mouth of an empty jewelry box that once held a pair of ancient pearls and the "something old" and "something new"

that were worn on a long-ago wedding day. My friend felt vio-
lated, angry, anxious, and unsafe in her home—a place that
should have been her haven.

That second letter made me feel burglarized too. Something
valuable was ruthlessly taken. I read the letter again and again,
each time feeling a new variation of trauma and anguish. When
I read my father's surname, I remembered how it had once been
mine too, before Mom had replaced it with my stepdad's last
name. I heard the awful sound of it, pounding in my mind.
There had never been a time when the name seemed natural.
Whenever I heard it or had to say it out loud, my throat burned
with the taste of it. I hated that I could never escape it. That
name had followed me into every classroom and doctor's office
where I had to write it down again and again, to claim it as my
own. It clung to me at all times, a verbal link that connected
me to a man who abused me and continued to play the role of
my father.

I rushed down the hall and into the office across from my
bedroom. I yanked the metal handle on my file cabinet and it
groaned open, heavy with car titles, insurance policies, school
certificates, old immunization records, and a stack of dog-eared
magazines with stories I'd written or intended to read. I plunged
in like the claw in an arcade game, tossing aside everything of
insignificance. When I found the blue folder containing birth
certificates, I tore it out of the drawer and pulled out the contents. Stuck behind my sons' birth announcements that bore
the tiny ink-stamps of their feet, I found my own birth certificate folded in thirds. I don't know what compelled me to open
it. The document sickened me. It was my second birth certificate; Mom had legally changed the first. Canceled the first
when she canceled my Dad. The paper was oddly crisp, a sterile
shade of white like a pair of bleached socks. Reading it was like

forcing my eyes on a solar eclipse. There, beneath my mother's maiden name, was the seven-letter lie that ripped at my insides and hollowed me out. I stood there, one hand on the cold file cabinet, the other gripping the document. If I were the victim of a home invasion, my mother was the reckless thief.

Against my better judgment, I still waited for some kind of acknowledgment, a word of encouragement from Mom when I called her during my lunch breaks. She talked about the new series she was watching on television, the promotion she got at work, and the expensive heart medicine her dog was taking. When I told my therapist this during our next session, it felt like high school gossip. I thought she'd repeat what Wes said months ago, after I'd invited Mom to our wedding. "I don't understand why you keep expecting a different outcome." I waited for her to tell me in a kind yet clinical tone that my behavior was the definition of insanity. I was driving myself insane. But she didn't say that. She didn't tell me I was crazy, needy, foolish, childish or self-absorbed. Instead, she explained the value of accepting my feelings and reflecting on the events that triggered my emotions.

"Self-validation. Have you heard the term?" she asked. "Very early in life, we learn to seek validation from our parents. Being habitually denied approval, acceptance, and support on an emotional level can take its toll."

"I understand."

I set my phone in my lap and pressed the speaker button. I cracked my car window and breathed in the smell of the damp afternoon. "But I'm an adult," I continued. "Shouldn't I have outgrown these. . . needs?" Parental validation seemed an immature thing for a woman to want. A forty-one-year-old woman.

"Independent people still need validation," she asserted.

"It's normal to seek it from those we love. It's how we build trust and respect in relationships. But. . ." her voice trailed off.

I took notes as if I were at work, as if I were writing a story about a woman who was out of her mind. I created a document on my computer with bullet points that highlighted our discussion. As I wrote, I searched for a satisfying ending, the one that looked best on the page. I wondered if playing reporter helped me see the situation objectively, or if I was simply avoiding my grief. Someone else's story was easier to write than my own.

For a full hour we alternately chatted and listened, and before the end of our session, the therapist shocked me with her advice. "I think you should limit your talks with your mother. How about a weekly or monthly phone call instead of every day?"

I sat silent. Mom's voice wailed like a siren in my head. I thought of her distrust of therapists, and the things she'd said in the past: *They're always blaming mothers. Psychiatrists are all the same.*

I resented my therapist for a moment, for villainizing my mother. How strange to be told to stay away from your mom. From childhood, we cling to our mothers. *Don't talk to strangers* is the first rule we learn. Yet there I was listening to a stranger, a woman who could be anyone at all. A serial killer, a bad mother, a cheating spouse, an awful boss. I thought of the double life she might lead, how she could be the consummate professional who goes home to berate her husband, neglect her children, drink bottles of wine in her bedroom. Why was I listening to this woman on the end of the line?

Family is the most important thing. Your mother gave you life. What kind of daughter cuts ties with her mother? I must be a difficult person, a whiner, an ingrate, a traitor, a deeply selfish daughter.

I looked out the window and saw a woman standing on the

median, traffic streaking around her. A delivery truck rumbled past her and I could almost see her body vibrate as the tires turned on the pavement. Life whirling past her. She looked like a squirrel trapped in the street, a tiny trembling animal. What kind of woman was I? I was a woman on a median. I wanted to cross over and be on the other side.

The therapist began again. "Are you afraid of confrontation with your mother?"

"Yes," I said. "I don't want to fight. I don't want the stress of it anymore. I can't handle any more of her rejection."

I thought of the letter I'd written her years before, the way I painstakingly poured my words onto the page only to have her throw them back up in my face and threaten to take her own life.

"You don't have to go into great detail," my therapist said. "Just tell your mother you need space."

I dreamed I was in my scrubs again. There was a patient in room thirty-two. I stood in the hallway, the overhead light spilling down on me. From the row of hospital windows, I saw a perfect circular moon, like someone poked a hole in the black sky. I pulled a pair of gloves from the cardboard box on the supply cart outside the patient's door. I slipped them on and crept into the room. It was midnight, and the patient was sleeping with her face toward the window. I saw the back of her head, her hair splayed on the starchy white pillow. I reached over and touched her shoulder, shook it gently, and told her it was time to turn over. Time to rotate her position. She was a small woman, and I'd done this with men twice her size: Lower the head of the bed, tug on the draw sheet, roll the body, tuck a pillow in the crook of the back, another between the knees. I began the process, but she resisted. She grabbed my arm with alarming force. Her fingers pushed into my forearms, her nails digging tiny trenches into my skin.

"I'm just here to help you," I said. She turned her face toward mine and her eyes flashed open, radiant like a pair of headlights. Suddenly, I recognized the woman: My mother.

For so long I'd been the caregiver, everyone's go-to girl. I let Mom's emotional well-being supersede my own. I heard the echo of patients past, felt the grip of their hands on my arms in the night. It was time for me to walk away, to tend to my own happiness.

This dream played over in my mind and jolted me awake. I conjured the image of my sister beside our father's hospital bed, begging for more time. I wondered if more time with Mom would only mean more disappointment. If our daily calls would only yield more of the same. Was I ready to walk away if it meant I could end my suffering?

I continued to feel restless at night, shifting from side to side, punching my pillow and kicking the sheet off then pulling it back over my body again. My doctor prescribed an antidepressant. I didn't know if the medicine was making me more or less me, but after just a few weeks, the agitation lessened. I resumed old routines. I sipped coffee, read books, and wrote stories on weekday mornings when Wes had gone to work and Sym was asleep down the hall. These quiet hours soothed me. After I closed my laptop, I pulled on my workout clothes and hopped on my treadmill for a two-mile run. I played songs that pumped me up and made me feel powerful, songs that left my whole body throbbing. Humming. When I finished my run, I rolled out my yoga mat and stretched into warrior pose. I felt free. I was a flag in the wind, billowing in the sunshine. This was my self-care routine, an essential part of my life. Lying on my mat, my heart thumping, I considered what the therapist said about healthy boundaries.

There was a time when chats with Mom smoothed my frayed nerves. On the lonely nights when I faced divorce, and in the early mornings when I needed her voice to pilot me through the snowstorms toward home during those winter months in Wisconsin. Now our conversations set me ablaze with anger and left me smoldering when we hung up the phone. I knew that self-care was work, but it would be worthwhile. My devotion to Mom had become a kind of self-sacrifice. It was no longer self-care. Instead, it bordered on self-destruction.

Mom's promotion left her swamped with no time for phone calls during the workday. We stopped talking for days, then weeks. At first, I missed hearing her voice. I considered her a friend, no matter how complex our relationship. But surprisingly, I felt better. Like an overworked muscle, my soul had been screaming for rest. I spent my lunch hours in my quiet car. I left the radio off and let down the windows. I read novels in the shade near a pond and paused to watch the egrets open their wings like white paper fans. When it stormed, I reclined in the driver's seat and shut my eyes while the rain pummeled the doors and windows in a way that made me feel cozy in the dry safety of my car, like a child in a homemade fort. I cracked the window and smelled the sharp wet air. All of these sights and sounds replaced the chatter I exchanged with my mother. Now I had Mother Nature. I realized that while I was alone, I didn't feel lonely at all. Instead, I felt relieved. Funny how her absence brought me this feeling. For so long, I'd wanted to connect with her. But drawing near only showed me how far apart we were. Like road signs on a highway, I read the distance in her words, and also in the things she didn't say. Between us there were miles of unspoken sentiments, apologies, confessions. My silent lunch hours took on a meditative quality, and life began to feel less chaotic. That is, until a bomb dropped.

Chapter 11

Surprise!

I was sitting outside watching Mia charge through the grass, her face flying upward as her nose reeled in new scents. The air hit me in cooling waves, perfumed with the fragrance of morning dew. Steam rose from my coffee like a song from the choir of my mug. I curled my hands around the warm ceramic as a bird burst free from a bush. I watched him become a little brown streak in the sky. In the forest beyond the patio, damp leaves glistened along the fence. My backyard was a freshly painted canvas, colors still wet from the brush of last night's rain. Amid all of this peace and serenity, my cell phone buzzed.

I saw a text from Sym's former girlfriend, a Taylor Swift kind of blonde who'd spent lots of time at our house during the years when they dated. The first time I saw her standing behind the cash register at the restaurant where my son worked, I nudged his elbow and lifted my chin in her direction as if to say, "What do you think?" He was sixteen, and soon after, they'd begun dating. She worked hard. I recall her rushing home in her senior year of high school so she could pull on her work clothes for the evening shift, a button-down shirt, black pants, and an apron. I hadn't seen her since they had broken up, and now she was on the phone saying she'd like to talk to me. She *needed* to talk to me.

Two hours later, she was standing in my kitchen with a baby on her hip. My son's baby—or so she said. Her name was Juli-anna, JJ for short, and she was three months old. When I asked why I was only just hearing the news, her face flushed and she shifted from foot to foot, patting the baby's diapered bottom.

"Sym and I weren't talking anymore. He blocked my calls," she said, and her eyes met the floor.

This made sense to me. My son was incredibly stubborn. When he made up his mind, he made up his mind. Still, I'd been around, available. I had never blocked her calls, and she'd always known where we lived. I wanted to tell her this, but what was the point? She was young, and shy, and patting the baby with a nervous hand. I thought she must be wrong about her baby's paternity, so we should focus on sorting it out. My son could not be the father. Could he?

I thought of their stormy breakup, the way Sym paced the room, his large feet slapping the tiles with each labored step. The way he yanked a clean trash bag from the roll and threw her things inside. "I never want to see her again," he'd told me. "Never!"

That day, he looked at me with a broken expression, and I'd wanted to piece it all together for him. I could barely contain the mother-urge to grab a broom and sweep up the fragments of his heart. Now he was panicked, wearing the face of a boy who just crashed a car and must survey the damage. I saw the infant squirming, her chin wet with drool, her little pink feet thrashing in her mother's lap. How could that fragile human be my son's child? My *child's* child?

JJ was blonde like her mother, but her eyes were dark like my son's. She was beautiful, a Gerber-ad-in-a-magazine kind of baby. But when I looked at her, I felt nothing but a small flash of hope that she might not be ours, the iridescent shimmer of an unpopped bubble—the possibility that still floated in the air, which was: this might be a mistake.

"You understand how this sounds, how this could be a rather big shock," I asked his ex-girlfriend.

She nodded. "Of course. Yes, of course."

"I just need the confirmation," I said. I sent them to the pharmacy to buy a DNA kit. It was 2020 and, for better or worse, these things existed. While they were gone, I walked the baby around the house, showing her all the mirrors and watching her study her reflection. We stood near the patio doors, and I pointed out to the yard.

"This is Mia's office." The dog pushed her nose against the glass, and when I opened the slider, she bounded out. This made JJ very happy. "You're a dog lover, too?" I asked. "You should know that Mia is the best. But watch out for that tongue. She's a licker."

We sat in front of the television together, and I snapped a few pictures of her with my phone. Something inside me wanted to remember that day. When Sym and his ex returned to my kitchen, we opened the box and spread its contents out on the table. There was a phone number, a website, and a pamphlet with simple instructions. They took turns swabbing the insides of their cheeks then placed the swabs into corresponding envelopes. I decided I'd like to be the one to ship the package to the lab. Then, we'd have our results in under five days. We would know if our lives would be intricately bound by the three-month-old baby in my kitchen.

There was an awkward silence at the table. JJ quietly gazed at us with her big, cartoon-character eyes. I thought of the little bird in the children's book *Are You My Mother?* As a child,

I read it on my grandma's sofa. I laughed when the bird left the nest in search of his mother, finding a kitten, a cow, and a car, asking each if he belonged to them. As the bird became more desperate, I never feared for him. He'd find his people, I thought in my child mind, as if by the force of some fate-driven magnet all the lost birds were destined to be found. To chirp and fly and form Vs in the sky with their migrating flocks. If only real life had storybook endings. I really wanted this beautiful baby bird-girl to find her flock, but was it so terrible that I wasn't ready for it to be us?

"It's not my baby," Sym said that evening. "I swear I was careful."

When Wes came home from work he prodded Sym. "*Were you careful?*"

Sym shook his head vigorously. "Yes. Yes."

I felt my hands gripping an invisible rope. The word "careful" was some kind of lifeline. But I knew better. I knew that *careful* was not a guarantee. A lot of babies had come into the world despite careful measures. An after-school special played in my head in which a stern nun delivered a speech to two pimply teens: "Abstinence is the only guarantee, Billy and Suzie. The *only* guarantee."

"This would be the worst possible thing," Wes said, and I knew what he meant.

I didn't want that for my son, who was far too young for fatherhood. I thought of all the years I labored to make ends meet, the night shifts at the care center when I was so ridiculously tired. I'd see patients curled up in their beds and think, *What would it take to land here for a night? If I could break a leg or an arm, maybe crash my car into a tree. . . .* I was so desperate for sleep, I daydreamed about accidents. Then there were the post-divorce years, when my sons were finally old enough for school, and I could get a full five or six hours of sleep after dropping them off. Only I couldn't, because there'd be phone calls from school: *Sym is on the playground and he won't return to his class. Sym flipped a table over, threw a book, ripped his math test, ate his entire bagged lunch during first period.* This was exactly the kind of karma I did not want for my son. And, truthfully, I longed for a break if I could get one, just an easy few years for myself. A little bit of relaxation with my new husband. Grand-babies are nice. But not now. Not *now*.

I was forty-one—too young for grandmotherhood. But I also felt slightly too old for it all, like I'd lived many lifetimes in the years I had spent finding my way, finding myself. Now that I had a grasp on things, I wanted to enjoy that phase of my life before I began diapering a grandchild.

Wes and I sat side by side on the sofa and zoned out in front of Netflix. The next day, I told my therapist about the baby. "I'm not ready for this. Things were just calming down. I just got remarried for God's sake."

While we waited for the test, I felt as if we were in some kind of limbo. We were riding a cramped elevator together, moving toward an unmarked floor. I was afraid of where the elevator might take us. I checked, checked, and rechecked my email, awaiting the lab results. When the message finally appeared, I opened it with a hard click of my mouse. It read: *Your testing is complete and the report is now available online. Please log in and enter your case number to access the results.* My fingers nervously tapped the keys. I opened the PDF titled DNA Test Report. There were three columns labeled at the top: Mother, Child, Alleged Father. Inside each column were numbers punctuated with other numbers and the occasional letters. I didn't under-stand the formation, the rows, and the foreign language spelled out on the page. But at the bottom of my screen, there was a box that said: Probability of paternity 99.99999998 percent.

I knew how these things worked. I'd seen episodes of the Maury Povich show. I heard his voice in my head now and imagined him reading the news to my son. *You are the father.* But somehow it didn't register. In a state of confusion, I found the lab's phone number and called.

"Hello," I said to the representative. "I'm just calling to confirm the results I received by email." When she asked, I gave her my case number, my user identification, and registration details. "So the results, the uh . . . the numbers at the bottom of my screen. . . . What do they mean exactly?" I asked, as if it was a reasonable question, as if there might be some kind of loophole.

The woman on the line was practiced and polite when she told me with confidence the answer I didn't want to hear. My twenty-year-old son was a father. With my laptop in hand, I burst into his bedroom and showed him the numbers. His mouth cracked open just slightly as his eyes scanned the glowing screen. He was stunned into silence, and I knew what he was thinking. He wasn't ready for this either.

The elevator thudded to a stop and the doors slid open. *Where the hell were we now?*

The DNA kit had come with a pamphlet and simple instructions. A toll-free phone number and a website. But there was no kit for us now. I walked around the house feeling like I was naked at my own surprise party. I imagined the banner on the wall: Congratulations, Grandma!

I considered Marie's advice again—lean on your husband. I desperately needed his practicality. "It'll work out," he said. "We'll work it out." But I wanted to know how. *How* would we work it out?

I thought about how I would explain the scenario to others, the questions they would ask, same as the ones that drummed in my head. Why are we only just meeting this child? Why do I feel like a character in a Saturday night chick flick. . . *Unsuspecting Grandma: The Story of a Secret Baby.*

I can't say why my granddaughter's mother waited so long to bring the baby into our lives. I think about the months we missed, all the events we didn't get to experience: the frantic race to the hospital, and that dazed and confused moment when reality hits you as the newborn child cries out, her voice breaking into the room like a burst of new light. The shock of finally seeing her in the flesh, swathed in a hospital blanket, pink cheeks ripe as fruit, glazed eyes pondering the swirl of hovering faces, the faces of the ones who would love her endlessly.

But not my face, and not my son's either. Where were we when JJ was born? Was I mindlessly cleaning windows or reading a novel in my favorite chair? Was I making a grocery list: spinach, apples, bread? Where was my son when his daughter entered the world? Pumping gas at the corner mart, or sleeping late with the curtains drawn? Was it a Sunday, or a weekday? The middle of the night or early morning, just as the sun slipped into the sky?

I could be angry for these months I spent unaware of her existence. The time I didn't get to adjust to the idea of her, of me as a brand new grandma. As JJ's mother, her parents and siblings prepared for her arrival, I went about my days not imagining this child, not dreaming of her the way I dreamed about my own sons, of their smooth foreheads and bright futures. In the months leading up to their births, I never stopped thinking of who they would be, believing that even while their bones were forming, their distinct laughter, desires and destinies were already a part of them, like so many seeds dropped into fresh soil. Even while tethered to umbilical cords, they were their own separate humans, unique and wonderful and surely a little awful too. In all the best ways, of course.

Would they play with toy trucks and hunt for sticks in the yard? What kind of books would they choose from the library? Books about space, superheroes, insects or animals? Would they like vanilla or chocolate ice cream? Would they giggle or cry when the dog licked the melted streaks from their chins? I pondered the size of their fingers, how I'd hold their delicate hands in my palm, study the wrinkled new skin and feel the silk and softness of it. Now I felt guilty for the way I'd met my granddaughter, ashamed of my initial hesitation. I wondered if JJ's mother felt guilty too. Or confused, or anxious, or nervous. Did she feel like a child when she held her child, a little bit lost and lonely, too? Afraid of all that lay ahead, all that would now be required of her, a mother? In keeping this baby a secret, was she somehow punishing my son for all the ways he broke her heart? None of it mattered now. It was time for us all to step into new roles.

I busied myself with the details, cleaning bottles, and surveying the diaper bag's contents. We had blankets, bibs, lotions, and creams, a container of powdered formula. By all indications we were ready, but only in a physical sense. When the weekend came, JJ arrived for a visit. It was like hosting a tiny foreign exchange student—a stranger. When I showed Sym how to scoop JJ up gently, I still couldn't fathom she was his daughter. I bounced her on my knee and it felt robotic. When her lips bloomed open like a perfect rose and she let out a peaceful sigh, I thought how beautiful she was, this child who was impossibly ours. When her body softened and fell slack into mine, I remembered the word *leaning*. I should be leaning on my husband, but this baby was leaning on me. It was an unimaginable turn of events. A Twilight Zone reality.

When it was Sym's turn, he handled her like broken glass. His face still frozen in terror.

"She hates this," he said when she squirmed. "She hates *me*."

Around 10 p.m., we had successfully rocked her to sleep. It only took four hands, a few dances, blankets, songs, and a bit of teary begging. I'd have offered her cash, but she just wasn't interested.

In our bedroom before drifting off to sleep, I told Wes we should talk to Sym tomorrow. But I knew I'd leave the talking to him. How could I tell my son it was going to be fine when I felt like it all went to hell?

The next day we were in the living room bouncing JJ. A nursery song played on my phone, and I held a lukewarm bottle and a blanket in my hand. It was feeding time. Sym watched me from a safe distance in the corner, still convinced his daughter thought he was Satan.

"You know," Wes began, "I thought my life was over when I found out about my daughter."

Wes was nineteen when his girlfriend broke the news that she was pregnant. "I was clueless," he said, shaking his head and laughing. I thought of his adult daughter, Ashley, her huge brown eyes and electric smile. She was a prime example of the best possible outcome: sweet, smart, loving, and successful. A cookie-baking doctor with an engineer husband. Wes didn't have to tell us how it all turned out, how his daughter had become his delight. How a strange, slobbering baby could be an enormous blessing. I forced a smile at Sym.

"We're all still stunned," I said. "Give yourself time to adjust." I propped the baby on a pillow and a blanket, tickled her neck and chin. When she smiled I felt a stab of guilt for giving my son advice while knowing I needed it too.

I sat at the kitchen table, scribbling in a notebook. I put my therapist on speaker phone next to a cold cup of coffee. It was two weeks since we had met JJ, and I still found myself internally wrestling. I told her how it felt to be a grandma who should be elated but could only pretend to have joy. I told her how it felt to be an icicle waiting to thaw. Praying to thaw.

"Embrace your feelings," she said. "You have a right to them. It's not healthy to say, 'I shouldn't be feeling this way.' It's understandable you're upset. There's been a lot of change in your life."

The word "change" reverberated in my mind.

"I'm not happy that my youngest son is now a single father, or that his ex-girlfriend dropped in with a three-month old baby," I said. "It's confusing and surprising, but we'll work it out," I said, realizing I finally believed we would.

I found myself thinking about my grandparents. How did they feel when their youngest daughter became pregnant at sixteen, eighteen, and twenty? Aunt Rachel said I was a finicky baby. My parents had moved from my grandparents' home to a bungalow two doors down. But every night with frayed nerves, Mom called for my grandparents as I shrieked and howled incessantly. How did I know I needed them?

"Grandpa would walk down the street to get you," Aunt Rachel said, a smile tugging at the corners of her lips. "He'd take you home to Grandma."

I imagined my infant self, curling into sleep like a purring kitten in Grandma's arms. Warm, safe, unconditionally loved. I thought of the time Mom convinced me to move my family in with her, that brief stay that ended so abruptly. I saw Mom tending to Sym in the morning, his fat arms windmilling as he lay on her bed. Her flawless red fingernails fastening his clean diaper into place. I smelled her perfume and the candle that flickered on her dresser. I'd wanted my mother to be a doting grandmother like my own. But on the night we left, she'd stood in the doorway watching our packed car disappear in the night. She never asked where we would go, or how we would manage. I never saw remorse in her face that night, only the wave of relief as I strapped her grandsons in their car seats. After that night, it was years before we saw her again.

Anger felt like something I'd swallowed, something that rotted inside me. I followed the thread of rejection that connected one memory to the next. Me as a wounded child in need of compassion, as a young mother with two sons, as a bride planning her wedding, as a daughter grieving the loss of her father. Once again, I saw what I could reasonably expect from my mother: rejection.

"If you need to feel anger to get to a place of acceptance, let yourself be angry," my therapist said.

I took walks through my neighborhood with Mia. I let her sniff every mailbox as we made our way down the street. I thought about childhood, parenthood, and the way the sun shifted behind the trees, revealing both light and shadow as we moved along our path. Those past few months had disclosed life lessons that way. In bursts of light and darkness. And now the truth was almost blinding. I paused as Mia nosed through the loropetalum.

"Loro peta lum," I said, recalling a conversation with Wes. Our evening walks were often explorations in which I pointed to a pretty flower or tugged a leaf from a bush and asked if he knew its name. He'd pause to examine the foliage as I waited for the answer, feeling a kind of pride for my husband whom I could count on to know such things. Having a name for a thing made it less mysterious. Names are the basis of knowing.

When I heard the term "mother wound," it sounded like something familiar. I searched the internet for information, and I learned it was not a clinical term but a painful phenomenon, suffered by the under-mothered—daughters of emotionally absent mothers. Many of those mothers provided a home, hot meals, and the basic necessities. But they failed to supply the most important thing: maternal love, the lack of which can create the mother wound, an endless pit of need in the soul of a daughter.

For so many years, I internally argued Mom's case. I tried to fill my emptiness with running lists of her good deeds: the phone calls, the gifts, her expert housecleaning and the ways she fashioned a home. But my emotional self went hungry. Starved. I wondered if anorexia was my wound turned inside out.

In *Psychology Today*, a counselor described the effects of the mother wound:

Insecurities: The urge to gain a mother's love and the feeling that it is fragile and can be easily lost.

Emotional disconnectedness: Difficulty speaking, sharing or relating to the mother on a deeper level.

Striving: Always trying to please and protect the mother, even at the cost of one's own happiness.

Feelings of loneliness, depression, anxiety, anger.

I had found the root of my anger, and I felt like a diseased woman who, after searching her whole life for a diagnosis, found it at last. Now, there was a name for my wound, and knowing it gave me a sense of relief. But with ownership also came responsibility, the job of healing. I used this newfound wisdom as leverage, a conscious awareness of the power I held. I felt I now had access to the wound, and the courage to probe its layers. It would take time, focus, and dexterity. A bit of magic. Self-validation. I drew upon the memories of my Grandma. I conjured her as if by séance, and she gave me the strength to rise.

What would she say about JJ? I imagined Grandma lovingly pinching her cheeks, squeezing her chubby thighs, and whispering a silly song.

I saw Grandma swooping in for a kiss and winding her fingers around JJ's golden curls. Her imaginary presence inspired me. Her passion for the role of grandmother made me passionate too. The more time I spent with JJ, the deeper my affection grew. I scooped her up when she whined. I felt compelled to protect her, make her smile, and shield her from every possible source of discomfort and pain. At night when she fussed, I wrapped her in a fuzzy blanket and took her outside. We walked up and down the driveway as I pointed to the moon and the stars. We listened to the sound of the wind whooshing through the trees, watched the ripple of branches and leaves as the cool air passed through. I whispered a Christina Rossetti poem in her ear:

> Who has seen the wind?
> Neither I nor you:
> But when the leaves hang trembling.
> The wind is passing through.
>
> Who has seen the wind?
> Neither you nor I:
> But when the trees bow down their heads,
> The wind is passing by.

We walked beneath the streetlights and I pointed to our shadow, the phantom of our embrace looming on the concrete in front of us. We watched our dark shape shift, fragile and unfixed like time itself. We were tangled up with her limbs around mine and mine around hers. I said, "You're the baby, and I'm the grandma." But our shadow showed us whole, and I couldn't see where JJ ended, and I began.

I thought about my sons, how we grew together through the years, how even now their lives were woven into mine. I thought about Wes. Five years ago, I couldn't have imagined us married, and all the ways he would change my life. The people I'd meet, the family I'd gain, the places we'd travel, the love and the life we would share. I stood in the street in front of our new home. A newlywed with a granddaughter.

It happened slowly, but quickly too. Love bloomed from a seed to a garden. JJ was no longer a stranger; she had become a kind of medium, and together we channeled my childhood delights. When I held her, the lyrics of old songs filled my mouth, songs my grandma sang. I thought of the way she enchanted me, whispering her lines so I'd lean in close to listen. The delicate scent of Grandma's face powder. It came in a pretty gold box and sat on the bathroom shelf, next to her wide-tooth comb and a can of VO5 hairspray. I didn't have to ask myself, *What kind of grandma will I be?* I already knew.

I thought of the way my grandmother forced dollar bills into my hand when, as a child, I made the beds or untangled her costume jewelry, a job she'd invented to keep my hands busy in summer. I made excuses to go to department stores, then I found myself wandering to the baby section, snatching up lacy dresses, little shoes studded with pearls, a stroller for afternoon walks, a toy piano, a pink stuffed unicorn, books with pop-out characters and fuzzy animals. Books that said *Guess how much I love you?* and *Chicka Chicka Boom Boom.* When JJ sat on my lap, I opened the books and watched her eyes register surprise. As I read the words, I guided her plump hands along the pages.

I bought her a plush doll with smiling stitched eyes, a ruffled dress, and pigtails with fluffy pink bows. I taught her to kiss the doll's face. She opened her mouth and lunged at the doll with wet lips and toothless gums, like a drunken little old man.

"Be a good Momma, JJ," I told her. "A very good Momma. And one day, you might get to be a grandma too—if you're really lucky."

I thought of the Cabbage Patch doll Aunt Rachel bought me when I was a child, how she showed up at my school on a Friday afternoon, hiding her gift behind her back. How I ran to her as she kneeled in the hallway wearing her stylish work clothes and ocean blue eyeshadow. When she presented the doll, I examined her in awe: cherubic cheeks, braided yarn hair, a red-checkered dress with eyelet trim. She came with a birth certificate. Her name was Cornella Maggie. In a photo Aunt Rachel took that day, Cornella and I are twins with thick pigtailed braids and big brown eyes. I thought of how I loved that doll, and how loving her was maternal. Hugging her, tucking her into my body at night, singing *You are my sunshine. My only sunshine*. Love would be my salvation.

I wondered when JJ would be old enough to recite from Robert Louis Stevenson's *A Child's Garden of Verses*, and if she would love poetry as much as I did. I thought of the cracked leather volume I shared with my grandmother, and it felt like I was with her again. She was alive in those books and songs, and I was certain she somehow shared my joy. My long-gone grandma and I were experiencing my granddaughter together. I was a new member of the matriarch club, and Grandma was showing me the job.

When I left the room to refill my coffee, I returned to find JJ feasting on the dog's tail. When I sat her up to admire her beauty, she reached for the hem of her dress and shoved it in her mouth, exposing her little body like some kind of pint-sized exhibitionist.

"Look, little missy," I told her, "that's not a good way to make friends. Have some self-respect."

I wanted to teach her all the things Grandma taught me. I wanted to show her how to paint her fingernails, braid her hair, write a story and refurbish old furniture. If she grew up to be a new mother, I'd sit her down with a cup of coffee and tell her what Grandma told me when I was newly married with an infant. "You'll always be my baby." She'd be bleary-eyed and in a haze, not knowing if she'd ever shower again without guilt, wear shirts that weren't stained with baby puke, or sleep a full night in peace. But she would cherish the thought of being someone else's baby, someone else's treasure. She would feel a new bond had forged between us, a sense of understanding for me, her Grandma, a veteran mother.

She'd ask, "How the hell did you do it?" and "Will I ever feel human again?" She would find comfort in knowing someone else in the world had been through the mud she was in and had come out clean and sane. She would think of all the times she wore me thin, and I'd remember my grandma walking the streets at dusk in winter.

I'd tell her about the day I'd gone to my friend Amy's house after school in third grade. We'd played dolls in her basement, her glorious basement with so many toys. She had enough plastic food to stock a grocery store—little boxes of corn flakes, cartons of milk, and pink plastic donuts. She had a doll house with lace curtains, plush sofas and wooden tables with doilies and flowerpots. I wanted to live in her basement where I could comb doll hair all night and cook elaborate plastic-food meals. I'd meant to stay a few minutes that day, to chug some chocolate milk and see her new sticker book. But time got away from me, and I hadn't called to tell Grandma where I was.

When I finally left Amy's house, it had gotten cold and the streetlamps loomed like bug-eyed security guards. I hurried down the street toward Grandma's house, afraid of the dark and ashamed of what I had done. Grandma was my after-school sitter and I'd stood her up like a bad date. When I saw her in the distance, she was wearing a button-down wool coat with front pockets that flapped in her haste. It was windy and she was limping because of her arthritic knees. She looked so frail to me, a shriveled version of herself, like she'd shrunk in the wash. My poor old grandma, hobbling down the icy blocks in search of her reckless granddaughter. I suddenly hated myself, my horrible, rotten self. By the time we reached each other, I was crying. Grandma's face was a hard knot, but it broke loose when she saw my tears. She put her hand on my shoulder and we walked home in silence. She didn't scold or punish me. Grandma ruled with absolute love, and it was enough to teach me all the lessons I needed to learn.

Now, as I pulled my precious granddaughter close, I knew I was holding onto what mattered—even as I felt myself letting go, shifting my focus away from the anger I felt for my mother.

Chapter 12

A New Story

JJ changed our family—changed me. We practiced impressive tricks, like how to balance a wet, naked infant in one arm while reaching for a bath towel. We tested our endurance and agility. When JJ was overly tired or gassy and inconsolable, we exercised our ability to work as a team. When my arms went numb from rocking her and my patience was shot, I hollered to Sym or Wes. "Your turn. I'm out." Most notably was the way this little being stretched the boundaries of our love and demanded we put the four-letter word into action.

You can't tell an infant, "Enough with the crying. It's not getting us anywhere. Couldn't you just be cute again?" You can't say, "You're being unreasonable right now, and I'm way too tired for this." So, we found ourselves giving, and giving, and giving, and cleaning poop and vomit and drool until we felt empty, abused, and insane. And only then did I look up and see the sweetest eyes imaginable staring at me as if I were a sunset or a star. In my stained T-shirt and dog-hairy sweatpants, I'd become some kind of messy, groggy hero. And I felt that all my life I only partially knew about love, but now I really knew. I'd skimmed the Cliff Notes, and now I was steeped in the novel.

It had been a while since I took that course on selfless love, we'll call it infant 101. To experience this again with my new husband and son was the ultimate surprise blessing.

JJ was stunning, with her pouty pink lips and big dark eyes, eyes like the cartoon Bambi. I saw Sym in her more every day. She was almost walking when we stood her up and showed her how to reach for her push toy. She grabbed the plastic handle and stumbled forward while we held our breath. Every time this happened, we became super fans at the Summer Olympics, cheering on our incredible star athlete. Wes took to calling her "Bobble," because of the way her head bounced around. He made silly faces at her and she was mesmerized by him, my peculiar zoo-animal husband.

We got her a walker, which was really just a vehicle for torture. When she saw the cat lying in a pool of sunshine on the floor near the window, she pushed her chest forward and propelled her little legs like Fred Flintstone in his prehistoric car. The cat wasn't smart enough yet to know he was a target. But when JJ got close enough to make him roadkill, he was fast enough to scramble away.

She became great friends with Mia. When Wes sat on the couch with a snack, JJ and the dog rushed over and scowled and drooled at his feet, sending him telepathic messages: *Share, share, share.* "The vultures are circling," I told him. And we'd laugh.

If I stood at the end of the hall and called to JJ, she zoomed toward me like a gust of wind. I sat on the floor in front of her walker and let her slap me silly with her baby paws. She liked to get a hold of my lip and stretch it out like circus taffy. It was a bit demonic, but I told Sym she was discovering the world.

"Babies learn through touch." I thought babies also had either a mean streak or a wonderful sense of humor. I recalled my boys in their baby years, how they rode on my hip when I chatted with a neighbor, a teacher, a cashier, or the teller at the bank. At just the right time, they'd reach up and pull down my top, exposing a boob or two to the unsuspecting party. This immediately shut down the conversation.

Everyone joined the JJ fan club. They showered her with cards and gifts. Aunt Rachel, Suhaill, and Nadege whipped up gift bags with baby blankets and infant clothing. Wes's family sent their gifts too: hot pink dresses and books that mooed, oinked, or had fuzzy animal characters. They began asking, "How's the baby," and "when can we see the baby?"

When Wes's birthday rolled around, I spent the morning fixing deviled eggs, a platter of chopped fruit, sweet rolls, and a tray of cheese and rolled meats. I simmered a twelve-pound ham in brown sugar—his favorite meal. Around 4 p.m., his sister, brother-in-law, niece, nephew, daughter, son-in-law, and mother piled into our kitchen. We poured iced tea and sangria and everyone joked and chatted. But an hour later, JJ woke up from her nap and the real party began. I passed her around, and everyone took a turn admiring her as she cooed and babbled and drooled. I thought about how it takes a village to raise a child, and these people were our village. As I watched Marie with the baby on her lap, tapping the glowing keys of a toy piano, I thought, *this* is family.

Sym learned to entertain her too. I told him we're all just here to put on a show. We are her own private troupe of clowns, and sometimes we'd play security guards too. Like when she grabbed a lamp or the leaf of a plant and attempted to pull the whole thing over, we had to give her a warning: *Miss, step away from the philodendron.* When she stayed up past curfew, we had to remind her that she was still a minor and she should really be heading to her crib.

175

She spent weekends with us, and sometimes visited on weekdays too. Sym and his ex-girlfriend were learning to co-parent, to communicate with mutual respect. When she brought JJ for a visit, I welcomed her to stay for a while, and some days we walked the neighborhood together with JJ in her stroller and Mia tethered to my arm. Some evenings I returned from work to find Sym flying JJ around the living room, a jet plane baby with her burly pilot father. In his early teen years, he'd been obsessed with voice impersonations and watched YouTube videos in his bedroom until he mastered the Mickey Mouse voice. Now he put that voice to good use, although JJ wasn't as impressed as we'd hoped. She stared at him, probably wondering why he worked so hard to be funny. Then he threw her up above his head, and she laughed. I watched, thinking, *that's it, Sym, put some muscle into it.* He'd mostly lost that look of terror, and it only returned when her diaper was full.

But the bigger concerns crossed his mind too. We were in the kitchen together when Sym said he'd been having flashbacks, images of his angry father. The way he swooped darkly through the house sometimes, like a bat in the eaves.

"What if I'm that way, too," he asked. "What if I lose my temper with JJ?"

I could commiserate with this—the fear of becoming your parent. It's a fear I'd wrestled with for years. To some extent, we're all distant versions of our mothers and fathers. It's a reality that hits us during parenthood, around the time we start feeling helpless and overwhelmingly frustrated with our children and with ourselves. Our mouths fly open and we say things our parents said. Or we catch ourselves being old and irritable, and we feel the déjà vu of our childhoods.

Then Sym's words took an ugly turn: "Why did you stay with my dad for so long?"

I felt accused, the way my mother must have felt when she read my letter so many years ago. I stood in front of the open dishwasher, unloading. I had to focus for a moment to keep the clean glasses from slipping from my hands.

"It's not so simple," I snapped. "Motherhood is not so simple."

We were silent then, the sound of our breathing like a low rumble of thunder between us. I remembered the chill in our home. The icy crack of fear we skated upon throughout Sym's childhood. Fear of my ex-husband's outbursts or, worse, of his absence and abrupt return. When he stomped away for a day or a night, I watched the windows, listened to the noise of traffic, cocked my head at the sound of him, like a dog behind a fence. When would he lumber through the door? When would a new storm erupt? It was like watching the sky for a cyclone. The marriage had ended years before I found the strength to let go. I realized I had to release my guilt, the urge to cling to second-guessing or wallow in regret. I told Sym I was sorry for my lack of courage during the years with his father, for all the ways I subjected him to pain. I told him I was proud of him, and that seeing him in his new role made the journey worthwhile. The joy of seeing his joy, and also his challenges too.

Some days Sym called me super mom, but today he was insecure. And when it came to insecurity, blame was a tempting diversion, an almost involuntary reflex. This made me think of the expectations I'd had for my mother, and all the ways I'd criticized her. She was the one I blamed for my pain. I recalled the old proverb about people in glass houses, and I knew I'd thrown my share of stones at Mom. In her defense, and in mine—in defense of all mothers, actually—I don't believe we set out to hurt our children. But it happens no matter what. In many situations, we're damned if we do and damned if we don't. Life is complex and nuanced. It's not as dichotomous as

I once believed. What remained to be seen was whether our good deeds would outweigh the damage we did to our children. Had we helped them in more ways than we hurt them?

There was one moment when Sym realized that his struggles could also be her struggles. He looked at me with an agonized face. "What if JJ has ADHD, too?"

"Then we'll know what to do," I said.

But secretly, I thought it was possible we wouldn't, and that's okay. We were all just learning as we go. Learning how to love despite all the obstacles. The parenting books told you how to feed, bathe, burp, and swathe your baby. But how you loved was up to you. It was never black, white, or easy. Often it was unclear how to employ the rules. Love was the hardest thing a parent would ever do. It was an endless sacrifice, and so often it felt like a shrinking of one's former self. Only my heart expanded, my capacity to feel love and pain.

I'd begun training at the gym with KJ. He was now a certified personal trainer. Although I had exercised for many years, I'd never worked with weights. Now I curled, bench pressed, and did butterfly sets. I felt strong in every sense of the word. Adventurous. I was ready for all new challenges. KJ showed me no mercy. During our sessions he worked me like a drill sergeant, and I told him he was a terrible person. A deplorable son. He laughed and said, "Keep squatting. Ten more reps."

His wife Anna became pregnant, and he'd chosen a name for their daughter: Maizie. When he told me the name, I laughed and sang the cartoon theme song, "Maisy, Maisy Mouse. . . ." He looked confused. "You got the name from the show we used to watch, right?" I asked.

"I don't know what you're talking about," he said, handing me a weighted ball.

"Maisy. The little white mouse with the alligator friend," I continued. "We read the books and watched the show?" He still looked confused. I was sad about that. I told him, "Those were really good times."

It occurred to me that we each have our own set of memories. Some that are lost to him and some lost to me. That made me think of Mom. I'd told her about JJ several months ago.

"Wow, what a surprise," she'd said. No questions, no further conversation on the topic of this new life, or the new child in our household. I didn't expect her to inquire about her great-grandchild, to ask for a photo or a visit. I'd stopped expecting. It was likely she'd never meet JJ. She'd never met Joey's children, and it had been more than a decade since she'd seen my sister's family. Our phone conversations had become rare, and I thought we were both happier that way. She sent me occasional texts about movies I might like or the new floor tiles they'd laid in her house. I had to respect that she was content with her life story and the home she'd built with her husband of thirty-five years.

I devoted myself to my home and family. Sym had enrolled in college, and KJ and Anna compiled their baby lists, researching the various types of baby gear, rocking chairs, and nursery decor. I would have yet another grandchild to spoil. I'd stopped focusing on heartbreak, on the mother wound. It wasn't that I didn't have pain or a sense of loss over the relationship (or non-relationship) with Mom, but I understood my role.

To have a mother was to have a safe haven, a place to lay your head. I thought of my pregnant self, of bodies being knit inside other bodies, the miracles and tragedies of life. The mother-homes from which we emerged. When my sons were babies, I watched them drift into sleep, thinking, *these little beings own my heart.* Since the day I became a mother, the daughter in me could not stop wondering why I never affected my mother that way. Wasn't I worthy?

Blaming my mother for my misery became necessary. It was how I made peace with myself. It was the only way to grasp a pivotal truth: her inability to protect me was not my fault. I was, in fact, worthy, and I had a right to be angry. My mother had betrayed me, and more than the sexual abuse, the betrayal was the most traumatic part. Ultimately, I had to accept that my mother couldn't fathom the trajectory of her actions. Perhaps this was true of many people who'd caused immeasurable harm. I reminded myself that Mom's failures resulted from her own internal fragility, and the way I saw it, it was no longer my business. Many days I thought I forgave her. I wanted to forgive her. Forgiveness was a commitment to personal growth, a kind of buoyancy. It was the ability to leave the past where it stood. Blame could put me in victim mode, where I'd forget I had the power to create a better life. Blame could prolong my suffering.

I told myself flawed mothers were the only kind. The stories were everywhere—stories of sexual abuse, dysfunctional families, and mothers who turned away. What I knew was this: I was not the only one. So many daughters had mothers just like mine. Like me, they straddled the love-hate line, stumbling from one side to the other while struggling to move forward. They searched for answers, for clarity. They spent their lives trying to reconcile the mothers who were their safe havens with the mothers who allowed their suffering. I was drawn to those living characters. I felt a kinship with the daughters who shared their stories because silence could morph into shame. The daughters who spent their lives pining for other mothers, clinging to school teachers and fantasies of women who baked, hugged, read bedtime stories at night. Women who walked in beauty, like the woman in Lord Byron's poem.

My mother had her own version of our story. Aunt Rachel told me about the years she and my mother worked in the same office when I was a child. Sometimes she'd overhear Mom in the breakroom telling coworkers about the weekends she spent with her kids, the family outings.

"I'd just listen, thinking, this never happened. *I* was the one spending time with her kids!" Aunt Rachel shook her head in disbelief.

I wondered if my mother's stories represented her true intentions. Did she want to be the mother she portrayed? In telling her stories, did she become that mother somehow? Were her stories a means to reshape our history, to rewrite a painful reality? Perhaps her tales made her choices bearable. They were her own kind of truth.

My mother had a right to her stories, whether fact or fiction. It was time for me to accept this.

I could not change the story of our past, but I could write a better future for myself and my family. Maybe this journey was not about mending my relationship with Mom. Perhaps it was about accepting her limitations and embracing those who were there to love me and teach me what it meant to be loved. Although I was not a numbers girl, it was easy to see how the math worked out. I could count more sources of joy than pain. One broken mother did not equal a broken spirit—not this time. I had a husband, sons, and a grandchild, and while I'd always be a daughter, I was also a matriarch. That was the character I would embrace in the story that lived in my heart.

I continued to write to heal, and I often thought the words that spilled out of me were not fully my own. Writing was a conversation, a trail of breadcrumbs that led to my inner world. I once wrote, "To be loved is good, but to be understood is everything." I thought I knew what that meant at the time.

Humans long for understanding, and in those days I thought I'd found it in my ex-husband. His fractured relationship with his mother mimicked my own. I thought that somehow made us two halves that could come together and be whole.

Later, I saw how the heartache had weighed me down. I told my adult self, *Grow up, girl. Move on.* But what I'd learned was this: You could change your address, your habits, your husband, your life, but you couldn't leave trauma behind. Trauma forged a wound; it lived in the body, and even healed wounds leave scars.

If one hundred things could make me happy, having ninety-nine felt like a curse. The one thing that was missing haunted me most. Pretending I didn't need it, that I had enough to numb the pain made my sense of loss grow stronger. But relentlessly seeking validation from Mom was a mistake. My therapist said acknowledging my feelings was a vital step toward healing. I realized how Mom taught our family the opposite, from the earliest days when she and my father divorced. She gave me a new dad, a new name, and a new identity. After years of my stepdad's abuse, she denied me the chance to grieve, to speak, to feel the emotions I needed to feel to get to a place of healing. My pain dressed itself up in the cloak of anger, an acceptable disguise.

I consider things Mom had the strength to give: clean clothes, hot meals, and birthday gifts. She rushed over the night the ambulance came to get Sym. She sat by my side when I wondered what I would do with a suicidal son. She wasn't eloquent with her advice, but she was present and she listened. She bought me the sweaters I'd eyed in store windows. She had a knack for nailing gifts, for speaking love with this particular language. There was something about the right material object that could make a person feel heard, loved. Mom worried about how I dressed in winter. As a teen, I tried leaving the house wearing flimsy canvas shoes, but she stopped me at the door. Holding a pair of fur-lined boots, she proclaimed, "Wear them or stay home." Mom was fastidious with those details. It was the larger things she missed. I could write a list of ninety-nine ways my mother loved me. But she'd failed to protect me from the sexual abuse from her husband, and failed to support me, and validate my right to feel the pain. Those were the things I needed the most. Writing about this after so many years felt forensic in nature, like a surgical extraction. It was me, finding the tools to attend to my wound. While I didn't respect the choices Mom made, I'd accepted them. Perhaps I'd learned the Buddhist concept of detachment, and was finally—lovingly—putting it into practice.

It was strange how heartbreak left me reeling. My father's death caused an explosion that threw me into the past. But it was a necessary journey. For so many years, I allowed my mother to reject me again and again because I gave her choices when I should have given her boundaries. My friend said "reparent yourself." I laughed, but she was stone-cold serious. She told me it was a method people used to heal their inner child, to go back in time and give their broken selves the missing pieces. With my granddaughter, I was finding those pieces, reparenting myself through the act of caring for her.

If I couldn't find healing in Mom, I could find it in myself. When I sat down to write, I practiced self-validation. I broke the silence through the immortal act of storytelling. I tried to make healing tangible, something I could reach out and grab, a million tiny bandages. I realized, they were everywhere. Healing was a song I wrote and sang to myself, the music I made when I poured my first cup of coffee with the swish of cream in my mug. When I lay on my yoga mat, healing came in the slow breath that filled my body, the exhale I offered like a prayer, a wish, a note of gratitude. Healing moved through my fingers when I found the washcloth in the shower, and the fragrant soap. When I lathered my body with care. Healing was a kindness, a cozy sweater, the sweet melting of chocolate on my tongue, and my favorite book. Healing was everything I chose or rejected. Healing was a process I'd continue, a matter of moving bad energy and replacing it with gratitude and joy.

For so long I believed I could find healing in Mom's love, in something she might say, do, or offer. Now I saw the error of my ways. I gave Mom the power I'd had all along, the strength and the will to nurture and protect my own heart. Within the mother wound, my body held the imprint of my trauma. But healing was attainable too. Healing was mine for the taking.

I thought of Lord Byron's poem "She Walks in Beauty" and the lines, "And all that's best of dark and bright meet in her aspect and her eyes." I once thought of only the physical features that embodied a woman of beauty, but now I know that beauty runs deeper. More than raven tresses and sweet expressions, it was strength and fragility. It was the balance of being and *doing* the things that radiate beauty. But also, it was the courage to say, "I was wrong and I'm sorry." These were the words I'd longed to hear. But more importantly, they were the words I needed to say. Because like my mother, like every woman and mother, I had been ugly and angry and flawed. But now, I have the wisdom to be the woman I've always needed—the woman who walks in beauty.

Acknowledgments

As with my first memoir *Petals of Rain*, this book came to me slowly, page by page. It revealed itself to me like a curtain opening to the light of day. I wrote as I learned, and the conversations with my therapist helped me sort through my emotions to understand the deeper meaning and the impact of unresolved pain.

I am profoundly grateful for the professional help and guidance, and for my therapist's vital words. I wish I could tell every person from every walk of life these words: Your feelings are valid. These words have stayed with me, and they continue to buoy me whenever I begin to doubt my right to feel any of the varying emotions a person feels after being denied a voice.

Abuse takes many forms. Mine was sexual, but what I failed to grasp prior to therapy, was that the bigger trauma I experienced came from my mother's rejection, her inability to feed my starving need for validation.

Not everyone will understand how childhood pain settles in your bones so that it is hidden below the skin and untraceable—even to the victim. If we are lucky, we are able to identify it later, and this is key to uncovering the mysteries of depression, and in some cases, physical ailments and diseases. Trauma is the master of disguise.

Some people will say what's in the past is so far away that it cannot possibly affect the present. Or that we ought to "let it go," as if we can decide to feel a certain way because it is the mature thing to do. *Put on your big girl panties, and stop all that whining*. I believed this was the right approach, but this line of thinking only made me guilty of the same emotional crimes my mother had inflicted. I unknowingly made an enemy of my trauma, which only held me back and increased my suffering. Embracing trauma is the only way to get through it.

The great Maya Angelou said, "People will forget what you said. People will forget what you did, but people will never forget how you made them feel."

So we see that feelings are seeds that become implanted in the darkness inside of us. We cannot ignore them without consequence. They will grow wild and weedy if left untended.

Whether we call ourselves blessed, whether we have fancy cars, houses and successful careers, we have the right to sadness. But as Miss Angelou also said, "A wise woman wishes to be no one's enemy; a wise woman refuses to be anyone's victim." In those words, I see my responsibility to myself and others. I am allowed to be sad or angry, but I strive to be healed. It's not okay to make trauma a weapon. Justice is an illusion, as it can never negate the original crime.

Now here's the part where I thank a whole lot of people. . .

This book was not written to hurt anyone, especially my mother, whom I will always love. I thank her for giving what she gave, regardless of what I felt I was owed. I thank my fearless book coach, developmental editor, and literary consultant Jill Swenson for telling me the truth without hesitation, and for helping me shape my work.

I thank my aunt "Rachel" (quotation marks represent names I have changed) for her unceasing support, and for making my childhood brighter with her constant love. I thank my sister "Jesse" for helping me when I struggled to decipher my memories. Sometimes memories can be elusive, and their distance can make us unsure of their existence as fact. Jesse helped me pluck them out and hold them up to the light.

I thank the friends who listened and read my work, and who will surely read this book from cover to cover. And of course, I thank my patient husband whose love and humor always lifts me up. His mother Marie, his sister and daughter, have always treated me like family. I write this with tears because your big hearts are astounding.

I thank my sons and granddaughters, whose presence in my life is as essential as air. The word love is far too flimsy to bear my feelings.

For my readers, I wish you all the good things that lie on the other side of trauma—may we all turn the page knowing that every chapter is ours to keep. Our stories are ours forever.

Sincerely,
Rica Ramos-Keenum

P.S. Some readers may note the addition of the name "Ramos," which is my given name. I felt it was important to include this link to the past. As I have acknowledged my mother's role, I wish to acknowledge my father's as well. Taking back the name feels like a rite of passage and a significant step in my commitment to self-validate. To carry the name that was stolen from me, along with my identity, is a gift and a constant reminder that I am indeed somebody's daughter.

About the Author

Rica Ramos-Keenum is the author of *Petals of Rain: A Mother's Memoir*, and *Nobody's Daughter*. She's worked as a senior staff writer for a media company in Florida, and is currently writing her first fiction novel. Rica loves dogs, books, yoga, and eating everything with chopsticks—because they're way more fun than forks. Find her online at Ricawrites.com.

SELECTED TITLES FROM SHE WRITES PRESS

She Writes Press is an independent publishing company
founded to serve women writers everywhere.
Visit us at www.shewritespress.com.

Poetic License: A Memoir by Gretchen Eberhart Cherington. $16.95, 978-1-63152-711-1. At age forty, with two growing children and a consulting company she'd recently founded, Gretchen Cherington, daughter of Pulitzer Prize–winning poet Richard Eberhart, faced a dilemma: Should she continue to silence her own voice? Or was it time to speak her truth—even the unbearable truth that her generous and kind father had sexually violated her?

Baffled by Love: Stories of the Lasting Impact of Childhood Trauma Inflicted by Loved Ones by Laurie Kahn. $16.95, 978-1-63152-226-0. For three decades, Laurie Kahn has treated clients who were abused as children—people who were injured by someone who professed to love them. Here, she shares stories from her own rocky childhood along with those of her clients, weaving a textured tale of the all-too-human search for the "good kind of love."

Being Mean: A Memoir of Sexual Abuse and Survival by Patricia Eagle. $16.95, 978-1-63152-519-3. Patricia is thirteen when her sexual relationship with her father, which began at age four, finally ends. As a young woman she dreams of love but it's not until later in life that she's able to find the strength to see what was before unseeable, rise above her shame and depression, and speak the unspeakable to help herself and others.

Fortunate Daughter: A Memoir of Reconciliation by Rosie McMahan. $16.95, 978-1-64742-024-6. Intimate, unsentimental, and inspiring, this memoir explores the journey of one woman from abused little girl to healed adult, even as she maintains her relationship with her former abuser.

Now I Can See The Moon: A Story of a Social Panic, False Memories, and a Life Cut Short by Alice Tallmadge. $16.95, 978-1-63152-330-4. A first-person account from inside the bizarre and life-shattering social panic over child sex abuse that swept through the US in the 1980s—and affected Alice Tallmadge's family in a personal, devastating way.

Secrets in Big Sky Country: A Memoir by Mandy Smith. $16.95, 978-1-63152-814-9. A bold and unvarnished memoir about the shattering consequences of familial sexual abuse—and the strength it takes to overcome them.